Ted Scheinman

Camp Austen

Ted Scheinman is a writer and scholar whose work has appeared in *The New York Times*, *The Atlantic*, the *Oxford American*, *The Paris Review*, *Slate*, and a variety of other periodicals. He lives in Southern California, where he works as a senior editor at *Pacific Standard* magazine.

Camp Austen

Camp Austen

My Life as an Accidental Jane Austen Superfan

Ted Scheinman

FSG Originals   Farrar, Straus and Giroux   New York

FSG Originals
Farrar, Straus and Giroux
175 Varick Street, New York 10014

Library of Congress Cataloging-in-Publication Data
Names: Scheinman, Ted, 1985– author.
Title: Camp Austen : my life as an accidental Jane Austen
    superfan / Ted Scheinman.
Description: First edition. | New York : Farrar, Straus and
    Giroux, 2018.
Identifiers: LCCN 2017038310| ISBN 9780865478213 (cloth) |
    ISBN 9780374712341 (ebook)
Subjects: LCSH: Austen, Jane, 1775–1817—Appreciation—
    United States. | Austen, Jane, 1775–1817—Criticism and
    interpretation. | Scheinman, Ted, 1985–
Classification: LCC PR4037 .S35 2018 | DDC 823/.7—dc23
LC record available at https://lccn.loc.gov/2017038310

Designed by Jonathan D. Lippincott

www.fsgoriginals.com • www.fsgbooks.com
Follow us on Twitter, Facebook, and Instagram at @fsgoriginals

1   3   5   7   9   10   8   6   4   2

For my mother,

and also for the most important Jane of all:

my sister.

She acknowledged it to be very fitting, that every little social commonwealth should dictate its own matters of discourse; and hoped, ere long, to become a not unworthy member of the one she was now transplanted into.

—Jane Austen, *Persuasion*

From this period, the intimacy between the families daily increased, till at length it grew to such a pitch that they did not scruple to kick one another out of the window on the slightest provocation.

—Jane Austen, "Frederic & Elfrida"

Contents

Camp Austen

Prelude: *Juvenilia*

From satire to sentiment

A love for books and mischief is often born in child-hood, and it seems possible that no child in English letters has ever had as much fun pillaging her father's library as the young Jane Austen; certainly no other child has left such a record of her resulting spoils. In her juvenile notebooks, Austen logs a series of literary performances in various forms that also serve as a reader's diary and a partial family scrapbook. Austen began these sketches around 1787, having survived two stints at boarding school, neither of which was a model academic experience. At the first, she and her sister, Cassandra, nearly died of typhoid fever, while the second was overseen by a one-legged huckster who claimed to be French and called herself Madame la Tournelle, but who in fact was an Englishwoman named Sarah Hackett. She couldn't speak a word of French, but the imposture of her exotic last name seems to have convinced various fathers of the gentry that hers was a school where their girls might learn the European niceties—the sort of school, as Austen would later write in *Emma*, "where a reasonable quantity of accomplishments were sold at a reasonable price, and where girls might be sent to be out of the way and scramble themselves into a little education, without any danger of coming back prodigies." The peg leg, at least, was real.

Instead, Austen's true education was in the family library, which she approached as a young marauder who marked her favorites with wicked parody. This period of artistic apprenticeship, beginning in earnest when Austen was twelve, includes some of the most vigorous short comedy in English prose. These days, to the uninitiated, Austen is remembered as an artist of manners, a prim moralist, a feminist avant la lettre, or merely a kindly domestic ironist—or more likely some mixture of all these. But in childhood, hers was a dark imagination, where she applied the cadences of eighteenth-century moral writing and popular melodramatic novels to narrating tales of viciousness and dissipation. As her family would emphasize almost to the point of annoyance after her death, the young novelist loved Alexander Pope's moral epistles and Samuel Johnson's moral essays even more, but the truth is she was an eclectic (and certainly not a squeamish) reader who devoured the bestsellers of the day, some of them rather lurid for preteen consumption. Like Catherine Morland in *Northanger Abbey*, the young Austen read French romances and all manner of Gothic novels, the juiciest of which were heavy on rape, incest, and grisly death. George Austen may have been a clergyman, but he was hardly censorious, and his daughter read what she pleased, whatever her siblings and Victorian descendants might claim thereafter.

Already as a child and teenager, Austen is said to have had a dry presence at the table, but in her performances on paper—and in her family's amateur theatricals—she was a swashbuckler. Her precocious ear for moral aphorism was matched by an instinct for the jugular. Austen would later describe her artistic range as a "little bit (two inches wide) of ivory on which I work with so fine a brush." Her line refers to miniatures, locket-sized portraits of loved ones, a metaphor for the ostensibly modest scope of her novels. Her earliest miniatures, though, are rather more like Hogarth illustrating Rabelais—wicked little parodies that use her father's library as a shooting gallery. Like rising authors of any period, she learned her craft at the considerable expense of her predecessors. Or, to quote the critic Frances Beer, "At twelve the little assassin is eagerly at work," satirizing the novels she loved (as well as several that she didn't).

Reading through the young Austen's notebooks, it's hard to escape the sense that, even at her meanest or most acerbic, Austen is always and everywhere a fan. Imitation is flattery, and parody is backhanded flattery, and Austen could not have written such delightful little hit jobs on Samuel Richardson and Eliza Haywood and others of her forebears if she hadn't read and reread her models with such voracity. In this sense, the juvenile notebooks—with their dedications to her sister, her brothers, and her female cousins—are a record of fandom: passionate but ambivalent immersion in a world of letters that she found equally ridiculous and intoxicating, and she renders this experience with such fine comic strokes that it's hard, even for a twenty-first-century reader, not to join in these perverse celebrations of her literary enthusiasms.

Like many young parodists, though, Austen soon outgrew parody, infusing the works of her middle teens with ever-more-realistic characters and situations. This shift from satire to sentiment was not simple (and never complete), but the notebooks remain a fascinating touchstone for anyone interested in literary fandom, and how the most flamboyant parodies are often the most affectionate. Fans of *Pride & Prejudice*, for example, will remember the first volume of the novel, where Mr. Collins makes a thoroughly uncharming marriage proposal:

> "And now nothing remains for me but to assure you in the most animated language of the violence of my affection. To fortune I am perfectly indifferent, and shall make no demand of that nature on your father, since I am well aware that it could not be complied with; and that one thousand pounds in the 4 per cents, which will not be yours till after your mother's decease, is all that you may ever be

entitled to. On that head, therefore, I shall be uniformly silent; and you may assure yourself that no ungenerous reproach shall ever pass my lips when we are married."

Yet Collins's embarrassing little homily begins to sound like Keats when we compare it with this, from "Frederic & Elfrida," which Austen wrote in her early teens:

"Lovely and too charming fair one, notwithstanding your forbidding squint, your greasy tresses, and your swelling back, which are more frightful than imagination can paint or pen describe, I cannot refrain from expressing my raptures at the engaging qualities of your mind, which so amply atone for the horror with which your first appearance must ever inspire the unwary visitor."

Collins is impossible without the earlier instance, but the earlier instance is also not possible without Austen's deep reading among the sentimental romances of her day. The assassin was really an apprentice, and the parodist soon turned her talents to something more lasting.

Austen continued in this vein for the better part of a decade, occasionally contributing essays and comic sketches to her brothers' literary magazine and invariably attending, or participating in, the theatricals that became a tradition in the household, after her brothers James and

Henry developed a mania for writing sentimental or satirical prologues and performing for the families of the neighborhood. The young Austen men found that the theater afforded them scope for flirtation and innuendo with the young ladies of Steventon, and the brothers used these plays and sketches as opportunities for bantering and peacocking—a motif that would later prove central in *Mansfield Park*. For her part, Jane seems to have been most interested in the comic possibilities of the stage, and her opus as playwright was a six-act spoof of Samuel Richardson's *Sir Charles Grandison*, a rather didactic brick of a novel that Austen cut down to size and ruthlessly lampooned. Like the rest of her work from the period, it's a virtuoso hit job, and the staged version reportedly took just ten minutes.

Those siblings and neighbors who gathered to watch the Austen family theatricals—many of whom are said to have cackled over the bravura comedy of the *Juvenilia*—stand as Austen's original fan club, reflecting Jane's own admiration for wit and language back onto her. It was a group that would expand outward from their Hampshire hearth to include, before long, Sir Walter Scott and the Prince Regent and, somewhat later, Emma Thompson, Kelly Clarkson, my mother, and, finally, me.

•

I dwell on these early squibs because they're important for understanding Austen, but also because they were my introduction to her writing, and for a long time the only work of hers that I had read. The *Juvenilia* was the extent of my Austen exposure as a child. This is highly irregular, and I might not even have opened that one, except that the Penguin paperback I lifted from my mother's office fit perfectly in the outside pocket of the backpack that I wore on the airplane that carried my sister, my parents, and me to England in January 1995.

That year, at the ripe age of nine, I was an American abroad, and like many insufferable Americans abroad before me, I was writing. My genre experiments included medieval romance ("The Selected Exploits of Sir Edward of Essex"), an unfinished abridgment of *Romeo and Juliet* in heroic tetrameter, and lots of truly terrible plays. We were stationed in London that year while my mother taught American undergraduates on a study-abroad program. It was an odd and abrupt sort of cultural awakening for me, and not just because of Austen's *Juvenilia*: when Mom took her students to plays at the Royal Shakespeare Company or some little fringe theater in Hampstead, my five-year-old sister and I came along as mascots, and soon I was mixing with London's theatrical set, some of whom sent their kids to the same wildly posh primary school where my mother's employers had established my sister and me. Many mornings, we would see Rowan Atkinson involved in the deeply slapstick task of delivering his children to the front gates. I joined the school cricket team and even got to play at Lord's, while, off the pitch, I enlisted my British classmates in a Shakespearean theater troupe and spent non-cricket afternoons writing with a fancy-feeling

rollerball pen inside a fake-vellum notebook, both pur-
chased with spending money at Waterstones. Somehow I
had absorbed the dangerous notion of the expatriate artist, and became utterly drunk on letters and London, certain that my alleged literary talent would soon earn the
rapt applause of a discerning audience. As with Catherine Morland in Bath, it was my first experience of being
surrounded by so much wealth and so much culture, and
it proved the beginning of an English fixation, one that
began with the theater and culminated, inevitably, with
an English girl.

Her name was Nathalie, and she was the daughter of a
well-known British actress, and already at nine she sum-
mered on the French Riviera and supped with the first
families of the realm; at school she was a natural gravita-
tional center, hopelessly cool, the first kid in the class to
discover the attractive posture of disillusionment. To me,
an ignorant American from dairy country in upstate New
York, the highlights of whose parochial childhood included community baseball games and the annual village
farm parade, she was a revelation. She was Estella to my
Pip, Titania to my Bottom, and she became the object of
a precociously faithful obsession that involved long-term
career plans: she'd be an actress like her mother, and I'd
write her scripts, and together we would rule London's
West End. While I tormented myself with such visions,
Nathalie seemed to find my scripts more useful than my
adoration. But she agreed to pool her money with mine

and my friends' to buy a theater where we'd stage a mix of Shakespeare and originals, and where we would also serve period dishes between acts, a sort of Tudor dinner theater. The food was Nathalie's idea, though she stated firmly that she was an actress, not a cook, and would never roast a capon for anyone. I promised I would honor her wishes, and that night I visited my mother's dictionary to look up what a capon was.

But of course, we had no money—we were young artists. Even after buying lottery tickets several weeks in a row we found ourselves no richer than before. Our most ambitious production took place not at the Old Vic but in someone's parents' flat, a masterpiece of compression that we titled, at Nathalie's urging, *The Ten-Minute Hamlet*. Looking back, one assumes Nathalie had seen a staging (or at least the script) of Tom Stoppard's *Fifteen-Minute Hamlet*—her mother was a regular collaborator of his—but, if our conceit was less original than most of us knew, the fact remains that we beat Stoppard by a clean five minutes. Nathalie insisted on being Ophelia, and a mock kiss between us, in the third act, marked the high point of my first decade—at once a literary and a sentimental education, and the first time I'd ever belonged to anything approaching a literary fan club—a circle of shared passion, dedicated to reenacting a previous age in manners, clothing, food, and love.

Around eighteen years later, I found myself suddenly involved in another eccentric literary fan club: the Jane

Austen fan club, its members known simply as the Jane-ites, into whose world I entered half willingly and half accidentally—and certainly with no idea of what lay in store. It began with a summer conference billed as a "Jane Austen Summer Camp" where, over a four-day period, from the opening plenary through the grand ball (where scholars and children dressed in breeches and bonnets spun together through the intricate dances of a Regency cotillion), I came to learn the rules of this secret society that has existed for two hundred years, now counts initiates on every continent, and offers seductions even to the skeptic. Following my partial conversion at the summer camp, my ambivalent fascination with this world would take me to several meetings of the biggest Austen conference of them all—the Jane Austen Society of North America (JASNA), where hundreds of superfans congregate to dispute interpretations, share recipes, peddle fan-fiction and petticoats, and argue with the finest scholars in the world. Throughout, I took notes on nearly everything, feeling sometimes like an anthropologist and other times like an embedded reporter, camouflaged in breeches. I didn't last in Austenworld, but for a time it was ludicrous, intoxicating, and sometimes heartbreaking—what began as satire progressed through sentiment and ended somewhere between the two. This book is the story of that trip.

Austenworld is a deeply self-referential and sometimes gossipy world—one, as Henry Tilney says in *Northanger Abbey*, "where every man is surrounded by a neighborhood of voluntary spies." My mother, Deborah Knuth Klenck, has spent four decades as a close reader of Jane Austen, and while she has never been a zealot for the costumes, she is somewhat known in that society for her academic essays and for her occasional appearances at JASNA conferences. Between her former students and her many friends on the Austen circuit, my mother has a bit of a fan club herself, or at any rate a wide network of correspondents, and these secondhand acquaintances lent me an instant credibility in Austenworld. They also served as an extended neighborhood of voluntary spies, who reported on my doings to my mother. Did I skip the dance rehearsals? Doze off during the lectures? There were phone calls on the subject. My mother is an exacting proponent of etiquette; as children, we were taught that if we looked or behaved shabbily in public, the shame would redound onto our parents, and to the extent that my adult conscience is capable of speech, it speaks in the register and cadences of my mother. The last thing I wanted was to feel like a supervised child. An inheritance is a blessing but, as I discovered, also confers duties.

But Austen gatherings are inevitably about family. Longtime fans who attend for the first time often attest to a feeling of homecoming, of meeting a set of like minds and like hearts. But fans also tend to arrive with at least some portion of their families in tow. Sometimes it's the sharp-eyed youngster who has read all of Austen by age twelve; other times it's the sister who prefers the Brontës, and who vents her spleen through mordant epithets; still other times it's the clueless husband, who has never been moved to finish one of the novels but who nonetheless submits without complaint when his wife insists on dressing him up, and who wisely defers to her on questions of Regency neckwear. Some parents bring their children to be indoctrinated; some children bring their parents for the same purpose. Without my own curious childhood I should never have cut much of a figure in Austenworld, and without my mother I might never have found my way in. But oddly enough, the crowning pleasure of my time in Austenworld was when I reminded my mother it existed. For years she had gone to these things only sporadically, and *never* had she worn the costumes. Now, I am proud to say, she goes every year, delivers a paper, and, when it's time for the ball, slips into an Empire-waist gown—and though her knees do not always permit a minuet, I am told that at every conference you will now see her at a table by the dance floor, a glass of punch in her hand and a coterie of adoring graduate students at her elbows.

Whenever one of my old confederates in Austenworld reproaches me for being absent, I can only respond that my mother for me is as favorable an exchange as they could ask. And then I promise to try to come next year.

ONE

A Shared Inheritance

A re you Mr. Darcy?"

The girl in short braids could not have been more than ten years old. We were standing by the registration table in a small anteroom, surrounded by a tweedy gaggle of tenured scholars and one or two graduate students. Posters of Jane Austen adorned the walls in silent observation. I looked down at this tiny and quite serious lady, whose expression matched her question: curt and business-like, the soul of efficiency. She might have been a private detective or a tax collector. A brief parade of women in sundresses brushed past us en route to the weekend's first lecture.

"Are you Mr. Darcy?" she repeated. It was a kind of accusation that had the momentary effect of silencing the company. "A lady over there told me you were." She stabbed her finger in the direction of the main room. A lot seemed to depend on my answer.

"Not yet," I informed the girl. "But I will be tomorrow."

She nodded, as though I had affirmed a long-held suspicion. "I told my friends that I would dance with Mr. Darcy. Do you dance?"

I decided to tell her the truth. "Very badly." The girl finally smiled but looked somewhat vexed.

"But you know they're giving dance lessons today and tomorrow, right?"

I said I did, and promised to be there, and to save her a dance at the weekend's grand ball. She nodded and introduced herself, shaking my hand with a worldly sort of professionalism. Just as I was about to laugh, a volunteer usher swept past us, saying that the opening plenary was about to begin. The girl went off in search of the mother she'd left unsupervised, and I joined the flow of people entering the lecture space, which the conference organizers had dubbed "Pemberley."

.

Such moments are representative of the year and a half that I spent in the world of Jane Austen fandom. They were also its best part. Throughout the bicentennial of *Pride & Prejudice*, Jane Austen's most famous novel, I bounced from one Austen extravaganza to another—observing, dancing, listening to and delivering talks—but for me the story still begins and ends with a single conference, a four-day affair in Chapel Hill, North Carolina, that introduced me to a world of which I'd been only dimly aware, and that I still have not fully escaped.

At the time, just a few years ago, I was teaching courses in journalism and English literature while doing graduate work at the University of North Carolina. My advisor, James Thompson—a compact, ruddy-faced man with an immortal smile, an earring, and a motorcycle—had decided to establish the Jane Austen Summer Program, known unofficially as "Jane Austen Summer Camp." James pitched it as a sort of quasi-academic gathering that could nonetheless attract the proles—the civilian enthusiasts who take part in the special universe of Austen fan-fiction and web series and bumper stickers and action figures, and who (James assured me) are capable of reading Austen as seriously as the most humorless poststructuralist.

The idea struck me as fantastical: a Jane Austen Summer Camp! Yet I didn't doubt for a moment that James and Inger Brodey, his colleague and coconspirator, would attract a crowd. Austen mania is simmering even in a slow year; for the bicentennial of *Pride & Prejudice*, the turnout was assured. American enthusiasm for Austen is (as I would soon learn) passionate to the point of obsession, and Austen is considered by universities, film studios, and publishers alike as a sure thing. And I was more than a little bewitched by James's description. The projected conference sounded dreamlike, a little unreal: We would dine together. Nearly all attendees would bring Regency costumes. There would be dancing. There would be a one-act play. There would be afternoon tea. There would be a harp. Maybe two. Fancy scholars would give talks, but so would costumers and graduate students and "independent scholars." The whole idea of a Jane Austen Summer Camp jangled with friendly dissonance. It managed to suggest Jane Austen at a sleepaway camp in the Catskills or the Great Lakes, winning the archery competition, fiddling with the reverse-osmosis water filter, and refusing to participate in kickball.

Hearing James and Inger plotting the weekend, I was impressed by their close attention to material detail: finding the right harpist; naming the four main conference rooms after the four main estates in *Pride & Prejudice*; ensuring that Inger's children had suitable costumes. And I was thoroughly seduced by the levity with which they approached this work: all giddy mischief. At the same time, I remained a little distrustful of anyone who would pay good money to spend a summer weekend wearing silly clothes and discussing the importance of (say) eighteenth-century agrarian philosophy in *Pride & Prejudice*. Who were these wonderful weirdos?

Most important, James and Inger said they were prepared to pay graduate students for helping organize the weekend. I was fascinated. I was broke. I was in.

•

A few days before the Janeites arrived, during preparations with Inger and James, it occurred to me that the camp would provide material for a light magazine piece—that I would in fact be crazy if I didn't sell someone an account of the imminent bedlam—so I e-mailed an editor, describing the juiciest bits of the weekend: the clothes, the dances, the period food and drink, the theatricals that the graduate students would perform. "I think they might make me dress as Mr. Darcy," I wrote.

The editor responded within five minutes: "OH MY GOODNESS YES!!!" Suddenly I had another role: I would chronicle the weekend as a surreptitious participant-observer and gossip collector. Already I'd been anticipating the event with bemused skepticism, and the assignment merely lent professional credibility to the semi-satiric outlook I had been cultivating. I was prepared to play dress-up, to observe a group of literary eccentrics, to be amused by them, and, having mined them for excellent comic material, to write an essay and be done. I was prepared to find everything ridiculous, and anticipated that by the end of the weekend I would be thoroughly sick of Austen.

This was more or less my frame of mind when my mother called. James had invited her to speak—they've been seeing each other at Austen symposia for a couple of decades, and are on friendly terms—but Mom was recovering from replacement surgery on one of her knees (the other would soon suffer the same fate), and she sent James her regrets while assuring him that I would represent the family "with distinction." I couldn't help but feel that she had overpromised.

On the telephone, as I described my excitement and trepidation at the weekend's approach, Mom informed me that having to use a walker had given her "great triceps"—"the last time my arms were this strong was when I was lifting toddlers all day"—and asked that I not disgrace her at the summer camp. She rattled off the names of all the people she knew who'd be attending; their credentials; their spouses' various eccentricities; what journals they edited, and what conferences they'd been blacklisted from—all with stern instructions that I was to be "presentable" at all times, and especially that I wouldn't forget to iron my shirts.

"I'm not a child, Mom," I said. "I can be trusted in company."

"Yes, dear, but you do realize some of these people have seen your baby pictures."

I groaned. Mom was having none of it. "Don't be silly; you're getting paid. I don't want to hear that you were aloof, or that you refused to dance. Remember that you're my *surrogate*—"

"—and you don't want me to sully the family name."

"Well, not if you can help it."

She extracted the relevant promises: that my outfits would be immaculate; my bearing, courteous and attentive. But I also pointed out that the summer camp might eventually lead to Austen overload. "What if I reach a point where I just can't take it anymore?"

My mother made a noise indicating contempt for the possibility. "It's just four days," she said. "You'll be great."

"This is *your* world, Mom," I said, needling her.

"You might just like it."

•

"We long for an age when people knew the rules of deportment, and followed them. It is a truth universally acknowledged that there was once a time when all children were well behaved and congressmen all told the truth."

James was at the front of the room in Pemberley, discussing the widespread idea that Austen's appeal depends on a kind of moral nostalgia: "Readers often claim that they are drawn to Austen by her sense of order, that conduct has rules and consequences."

It was the opening talk, titled "Manners Envy," and had all the markings of a hit for this crowd. The day was also very hot, the kind of hot where you start reading your own suffering into other people. We were in the great room in one of the university's more extravagant brick piles. Many in the audience raised a Regency-style pocket fan against the late-afternoon sun declining through the French windows. The thick heat of a Carolina summer pressed in. Some removed their bonnets, and more than one man loosened his collar; ties were rare, and became rarer as the talk proceeded. A trio of older women laughed over a photograph, then silenced one another, rapping each other on the knuckles with fans and brochures. A row ahead of them, the girl in short braids maintained a stoic impression, as though willing herself to forbear the juvenile behavior of her neighbors; a row ahead of her, I spotted one of my mother's spies.

Toward the front of the room, congregated beside

and behind the lectern, sat a handful of people who could only be professors of English literature, and who spent the moments before James's talk behaving like school-children reunited after a very long break as they laughed at private jokes likely hatched decades ago in a room—and on an occasion—much like this one. Certain women, defiant of the heat, kept bonnets glued to their heads, and no one looked more serious than the gentleman at the rear with muttonchops framing a face as pink as a grape-fruit, apparently having struck a compact with the heat that his soul would sooner depart this earth than the tie from his neck.

Even those accustomed to academic conferences and the eccentric specimens of humanity they attract would find this crowd unusual. The room was divided in dress: the majority wore twenty-first-century attire, but a seri-ous contingent was already repping Regency outfits, and some of the more daring attendees wore the fashions of the 1780s and '90s, when Austen began her literary ap-prenticeship and came of age. A scholar of colonial eco-nomics in the English novel sat between a middle-schooler and an amateur haberdasher; the latter identified as a Marxist and, that evening, would explain to me in pas-sionate terms the political history of the top hat.

From my seat toward the rear of the room, I scanned the backs of heads or sides of faces, playing a sort of bingo: *Duke*; *Arkansas*; *oof, there's [redacted], whom I've been warned about*; *to her left that nice dude from the German Department, and the gentleman who's delivering a seminar on "the female gaze in* Pride & Prejudice*"; there's the New York State contingent, and Susan, who edits* Persuasions, *and, yesss, the lady who published the funny paper on* Sanditon. The heroine in Austen's *Persuasion* at one point complains privately of a gathering "too numerous for intimacy, too few for variety." Based on my initial reconnaissance, the Austen summer camp would be both deeply intimate and wildly heterogeneous: even among these few dozen people (fewer than eighty, certainly), there was variety to tire the most energetic collector. There were the creamers, the fan-fictioners, the cosplayers, the tea makers, the Tarot readers, the Frenchmen, the bridge players, the hip-hop fans, the Girl Scout, the professors, the middle school teachers, the computer programmers, the law school students, the former punk rockers, the motorcycle freaks, the secret Victorianists, the graphic novelists, the Austen bloggers.

And it wasn't hard to pick out the core graduate students—the rank and file, ready for a weekend of buttling and scuttling. There was Emma, who would soon charm the throngs with her talk about *The Lizzie Bennet Diaries*, a web series that retells *Pride & Prejudice* through the conceits of twenty-first-century social media. There was Michele, of the chestnut curls, who would play Jane in our theatricals. There was Ashley, a born-again Christian who writes about communities of English evangelism in novels of the eighteenth and nineteenth centuries, and who was in one sense *living* the plot of a Regency romance, having just

gotten married—following a five-day engagement—
when her equally Christian husband was suddenly recalled to his post in the armed forces. Then there was
Adam, one of those beautiful souls who was probably
born scribbling a footnote, an ageless academic with the
ageless academic's traditional boyish gravitas. At twenty-
seven, with his wire-rim spectacles, an unself-conscious
grin, and the western fedora that he wore with his trench
coat whenever it rained, Adam presaged the way he
would look at forty-seven and at sixty-seven.

James's voice continued from the front, and his ready
audience tittered at even the simplest quip: "The novels
are undeniably social—Elizabeth is unimaginable on
Crusoe's island . . ." The beauty of that sentence is that it
instantly disproves itself—everyone in the crowd *immediately* imagines Elizabeth on Crusoe's island, and the image feels somehow in keeping with the idea of the entire
weekend.

Before launching into "Manners Envy," James had
convened the weekend with a short and awfully sweet
speech thanking all the necessary people and institutions
but mainly stressing the conference's democratic impulse:
you are welcome here, James intimated, whether you have
a Ph.D. or not; there are many ways to study Austen, and
no one will make you feel stupid for not "doing" Austen
in the sanctioned way. He further suggested that next year's
gathering would focus on *Sense & Sensibility*, and floated
the idea of one day holding a summer camp about "Aus-

ten and the Brontës." It was a bold suggestion—Austen partisans and Brontë partisans are famously opposed—and the crowd caught its breath in shock. (He also expressed gentle alarm over the suspected presence of "crypto-Trollopians" in the audience, a joke that landed with surprising force.)

James's voice was devotional and studiously subdued, as though apologetic for the enthusiasm it worked so hard to efface; in dress, James had honored the gravity of the occasion by abjuring his extensive collection of novelty Jane Austen T-shirts in favor of a casual blazer. He looked ecstatic, and rumpled, in equal measure, and once you know James those little rumples in his appearance take on the quality of something earned through honest labor. There are stylish academics and rock-star academics and antisocial academics and hair-tearing academics and bomb-throwing academics and so on, and then there are academics like James, whose professional status (lofty) seems to exist in precise disproportion to their vanity (indiscernible), with the result that James now goes through life looking accidentally distinguished and deeply tickled by the whole affair.

The room remained rapt throughout this little convocation.

"'We lead, as it were, a double, or if one will, a halved existence,'" James recited, quoting the sociologist Georg Simmel. "'We live as an individual within a social circle, with tangible separation from its other members, but also as a member of this circle, with separation from everything that does not belong to it.'" James's point was that we emulate or inherit social tendencies, and that Austen's characters must all, in one way or another, sort out their behavioral inheritance. I thought again of my mother, and of the attendees that weekend who would report back to her, and began to feel nervous.

•

James was concluding his talk with those wonderful rolling sentences that have the footnotes built in—the understanding being that even once we've finished the main business of the sentence, there are whole realms of literature to invoke in a series of nested relative clauses that qualify or embellish the conclusion with a series of knowing jokes, one of which might pertain to Thackeray, another to Mick Jagger—indeed, James tells us, he fears he is beginning to sound like that rambling woman in *Emma*—and the room leans forward at each parenthesis and subordinate clause, willing the words out. It felt quite unassuming, this opening paper, but it also held all the weekend's possibilities within it. James had presented new scholarship, in which he posited Austen as a foundational figure in sociology (a version of "Manners Envy" would appear in a celebrated book that he published in 2015), and he had done so to a "mixed"—that is, civilian and academic—audience. And he had also served as master of ceremonies and as court jester, while offering a melody for the gathering, a motif of sociability and the not unserious question of whether we can redeem our-selves in one another.

The audience, with all its motley energy, ate it up, as-senting eagerly to facts and assertions that would baffle any other room. James "reminded" us that the word "civility" appears seventy-nine times in *Pride & Prejudice*; most people nodded, except for one woman who imme-diately shot her gaze into a paperback, as though checking his math. It struck me at this point that the crowd was utterly giddy—people were snorting from the unrestrained laughter of belonging, and the little girl who was eager to dance with Mr. Darcy kept looking up at the woman who was clearly her mother to see if she was getting the jokes. The degree of excitement was frankly embarrass-ing, or would be to most adults on most days in almost any circumstance. James Thompson is not a rock star (even if he probably rode here on a motorcycle). But to these people, at that moment, James was in the flattering position of being the opening act for Jane Austen. And they loved him. When James stumbled at one point, beg-ging pardon for his "afternoon aphasia," audience mem-bers proved more than happy to supply character names *alto voce*: "Miss Bates!" "Yes, I believe—" "Miss Bates indeed." "Quite right." "—in *Emma*!"

I scrawled in my notebook: "Democratic conferences invite mutiny."

Two searching pairs of eyes will inevitably find one another, and as I rose to leave Pemberley, a broadly grinning woman from the New York contingent thrust her hand in my direction. A brief glance at her nametag confirmed that she was an acquaintance of my mother's and, what was more, a regional coordinator for the upstate New York chapter of the Jane Austen Society of North America.

"Is it—Miss Marie Sprayberry?" I asked. (The Henry Fielding–est moment of my life.)

"And Mr. Scheinman!" She shook my hand with vigor and leaned in with noddings of the head, which I learned was her way of sharing confidences. "You do your mother proud. I see you will chair 'Austen and Romance'?"

"So they tell me."

"And you are a guest film critic on the plenary about the adaptations?"

"I am."

"Well, I can't say how excited we all are"—indicating a smiling cabal of upstaters—"to be here, and I only wish your mother's poor knees had permitted her to attend."

"That's very kind of you. I'm ashamed to say I think you see her more than I do."

"I assure you," Marie said, actually producing and unfurling a fan, "I will send her a full report, on all aspects of the weekend."

I had no doubt she would—though I could not have known that this report would cause me some small trouble.

There exists a category of citizens best described as
Janeites-for-life, a scattered band of acolytes who troop
around the country and jet-set to London or Bath or
Mumbai or Tokyo, luggage bursting with petticoats and
paperbacks and Norton editions and hand-annotated
Event Schedules and endless spools of laminated name-
tags. They attend the big annual Jane Austen Society of
North America meeting, but they also bop through a less-
trafficked circuit that, if one has the stamina, need never
end. There is always another symposium at the local chapter of JASNA, or a talk by a professor at a nearby university
on "Austen and the Real Housewives of Uppercross," or a
screening of the Bollywood smash *Bride & Prejudice*. Like
members of any secret society, they can identify each other
through subtle or silent codes, and initiates all carry their
motley badges of membership in the global Austen circle,
from novelty pens to silk-screened T-shirts (KEEP CALM
AND FIND MR. DARCY) to playful indicators embedded
in e-mail addresses: ElinorDash1811@BartonCottage.net
will inspire trust among all similarly devoted correspondents. They come to laugh and to learn, to dance and to
listen, to admire and to be admired, to teach and to be
taught, to question their assumptions about Jane and to
confirm them.

The democracy of Austen gatherings is the thrilling
and disarming (and only slightly anarchic) secret of it all.
The snobberies of the high academy toward hobbyists,
emulators, and people so prosaic as to look for a *moral* in

a story resolve themselves, or go briefly on sabbatical. The guiding principle of such gatherings is the *yes-and* of improvisational comedy. If a gentleman raises his hand during a question-and-answer session and offers, instead of a question, a winding and irrelevant homily on the author and actress Elizabeth Inchbald, the speaker will acknowledge the offering and thank him for it and find a way to navigate back to the subject at hand without any deprecation. This is not to say that judgment suspends itself at an Austen gathering—far from it; there will be whispered remarks about that gentleman over supper— but merely that an attitude of expansive inclusivity is the foundational premise. Such is the hospitality prescribed in the novels, and such is the shared delight among people who otherwise would remain utter strangers, that resentment and unpleasantness achieve only brief, and rare, appearances. The Janeites would not have it otherwise.

There is something rarer, too, made possible in the society of the Janeites: an evenhanded commerce between representatives of the academy and their civilian counterparts, whereby the professors do honest trade with the costumers, and the costumers in turn are scrupulous in attending talks and panels. In many cases, thanks to the air of camaraderie and a general mash-up of eighteenth- and twenty-first-century fashion, the distinctions tend to blur. On one particularly embarrassing occasion, I stood for a full quarter of an hour next to an elegant lady in bonnet and gloves before recognizing that this woman was in fact a prestigious professor and close friend. We laughed over it, because where else would you glance at someone and say, "Oh, just another person dressed as Henrietta Musgrove"?

Some are born Janeites, some achieve Janeism, and some have Janeism thrust upon them. My own case is an amalgam of all three propositions. My full Christian name, Edward, will indicate my mother's Anglophilia, but when I tell you my sister's name is Jane there can be little mistaking the matter. My mother recalls two of our conversations during my sister's gestation. In one, Mom is lying on the couch, telling me she needs a nap. "Mommy's a little tired," she says. "Mommy's a little pregnant," I respond. In the second, she is at her desk and I approach, the miniature portrait of a snotty undergrad during office hours. "You love Jane Austen," I say, with a note of accusation.

"So?"

"So if it's a girl you should name it Jane."

•

One of my sister's friends recently asked her if she had been named for the novelist. Omitting the secondary consideration that Jane is also a family name, my sister admitted this to be the case. The friend offered a sunny observation: "Well, it could have been worse; she could have named you Fanny!"

"You don't know how close you are to the truth," Jane replied.

Fanny was the family dog.

My mother, indeed, could hardly have groomed me better for Janeism. A professor of English at a very small private university in upstate New York, she has been teaching and writing about Austen for nearly forty years. (Mom is, bless her heart, a neoclassicist, and what she lacks in conventional Austen elitism she more than recoups in distaste for the Brontës.) Under her tutelage, I was raised on a partial survey of the Brit Lit canon. One particularly painful moment found me in tears at the tender age of ten when, upon rereading the last chapter of *David Copperfield*, I became convinced that I would never find my Agnes, much as Dickens often despaired that he would never marry his wife's sister. (He didn't.) When we lived in England, before I had read much Austen or had any notion of the ongoing fealty she inspired, I was dragged along to see Austen's plaque in Poets' Corner at Westminster Abbey, and the little Chawton cottage where Austen spent so many years, and even her grave in Winchester Cathedral. For a brief period, any childhood illness experienced by my sister or me was treated with six installments of the 1995 BBC *Pride & Prejudice*, plus DayQuil to taste.

Austen was so pervasive that I rarely picked up one of the novels; at thirteen, I began my first, *Mansfield Park*, probably her oddest and least popular, and I enjoyed it without too much reflection, noting the narrator's general distrust of charm and her satisfying instinct for retri-

bution. My sister and I were similarly aware, in a dim
way, of the larger Austen world in all its finery, but our
contact with it was limited. I would notice a Jane Austen
action figure in Mom's office (packaging materials: "comes
with writing desk and quill pen!"), sent by a former undergraduate mentee who had contracted my mother's affection for Austen—an affection that defends itself with the
tools of lampoon: the placement of that action figure on a
bookshelf says, "Yes, I am inordinately fond of this curious
author, and yes, the very idea of Austen-as-superhero is delightfully absurd, and I'm acknowledging that absurdity
by displaying her action figure *pristine in the box*, as though
it were a collectible Batman doll or something, when in
fact this figure has no grappling hook nor freakish mus-
cle definition; her superpower is the ability to sit at a desk
with a quill pen, which is both hilarious and the greatest
superpower of all. I am quite serious about all of this, and
quite aware of how frivolous it might seem to the uninitiated, and I make no apology."

I think I also understood the impulse to apologize, or
to roll one's eyes at the Janeites. How else to explain the
strong note of accusation in my suggestion that Mom
name my sister Jane? It was an accusation of weakness, of
predictability. Even at four years old, a boy in America
has learned not to trust the softer, womanly enthusiasms
of Janeism; if I had been somewhat precocious in terms
of reading, I was at least equally precocious in reflexive
anti-Janeite misogyny.

One way or another, I made it to university without ever reading *Pride & Prejudice* and thought very little about Austen until I found myself at age twenty-five suspending a career in journalism to study political literature of the early eighteenth century at the University of North Carolina. My advisor was James, an authority on Austen who does not fit the Janeite stereotype. First, he is male. Second, he commutes to campus on a sleek motorcycle, which, in the summer, also takes him through the Black Hills of South Dakota and other rugged, windswept places on America's frontier. If someone requested proof that serious Janeism can coexist with serious emblems of masculinity, I would proffer James as Exhibit A. You know those THIS IS WHAT A FEMINIST LOOKS LIKE T-shirts? I have always wanted to make one for him that says THIS IS WHAT A JANEITE LOOKS LIKE.

When James taught Austen's *Juvenilia* and six novels to a small group of doctoral students in our third year, he also used the occasion to recruit us. Under his and Inger's supervision, a troupe of us agreed to spend part of May and June launching the four-day "Jane Austen Summer Camp," with the basic rules I have described: we would welcome lay readers as well as professional scholars, the food would be good, the punch would be fortified, and the dancing would rival that of any of the film adaptations. James and Inger had been planning to launch a yearly Austen camp ever since reading Jill Lepore's 2011 account in *The New Yorker* of her visit to the "Dickens Universe," a weeklong conference-slash-celebration that has been a fixture for more than three decades at the University of California in Santa Cruz. As he read about this learned extravaganza, James told me, "It sounded wonderful—as it says in the books, this darted through me with the speed of an arrow, that *we should do this with Austen*."

As James put it, after he and Inger returned from a scouting expedition in Santa Cruz: "It has an entirely different feel from a regular, professional conference, where everyone's trying to discourse at the highest intellectual levels—the Dickens camp does that, in what the philosophers would call ordinary language. So high-level, sophisticated, very subtle arguments can be made without jargon, without technical terminology, without endless genealogies of critical points and so on and so forth. And I loved that concept—it seemed a great opportunity for people who spend their lives in the library to learn how to talk to normal people again."

Austen is the rare sort of author who makes possible this unaccustomed exchange between academics and civilians; those who think of her as primarily a domestic novelist might be surprised at the extent to which Austen is able to kick scholars out of their armchairs and into action. Throughout the short summer camp, and for a long time thereafter, concerned friends would get in touch via social media, responding with a mix of mockery and alarm to a profusion of photos in which I was dressed like an early-nineteenth-century gentleman. One of my favorites came from my friend Max in Los Angeles, when he heard I was embedded with the Janeites: "Oh man, here I thought you were just reading Latin all day," he said. "Turns out you're reporting directly from the trenches!"

It was a lovely compliment, and Max's little note set off a bell that he could not have anticipated. There is, in England, a proud tradition of reading Austen during times of war, a tradition that became something like gospel during World War I, when, along with so many of his generation, one promising young scholar decamped from his armchair to mix with enlisted men and fight the Central Powers. In his bag could be found sodium tablets, instant tea, a few packets of cigarettes, and the complete works of Jane Austen, of whose literary estate he would soon become a sort of unofficial executor.

R. W. Chapman spent July 1918 on the left bank of the Vardar River in Macedonia, shooting Bulgarians, reading Samuel Johnson, and thinking very seriously about Jane Austen. In literary circles, Chapman already constituted a big gun: A star classicist from a young age, he had won the Gaisford Prize for Greek prose in 1903 while still a student at Oriel College, Oxford. By 1906, he was assistant secretary at Oxford's Clarendon Press, where he helped launch the Oxford English Texts series, establishing authoritative versions of writers deemed central to

British civilization. In the following years, he would become one of England's most ambitious lexicographers, write learned but amiable essays for *The Times Literary Supplement* on authors ancient and modern, and pay his court to Katharine Metcalfe, a fellow admirer of Austen who was an assistant tutor at Oxford and had edited the Clarendon Press's 1912 edition of *Pride & Prejudice*. In 1913, they wed—a partnership both romantic and scholarly, one that would reward all future readers of Jane Austen. If you're reading *Sense & Sensibility* in paperback—really, in any edition that postdates 1923—you're almost certainly reading the Chapman-Metcalfe version.

Though his primary project during the Vardar front was an edition of Johnson's travel journals, Chapman was also beginning collations for his eventual editions of Austen, including a supposed restoration of Austen's texts—plus notes elucidating matters political, religious, and military—and would write the occasional mordant essay from Macedonia to castigate previous dabblers in the Austen canon: "The writer has seen the late Dr. Verrall's copies of Jane Austen (modern reprint) and compared his marginal suggestions with the original editions. Some of them seemed to be unnecessary; of those which seemed probable, almost all were to be found in the readings of the first edition." Even at the front, Chapman kept burrowing in his books, seeking some more authentic contact with Austen. As for many Englishmen fighting abroad in the Great War, the nation's literary canon—and Jane

Austen in particular—offered a reminder of home, of what England was fighting for. And back in Oxford and London, Austen's clarifying reminder of English virtue sparked a reshaping and expansion of her popularity. In the first decades of the twentieth century, England herself was feeling "manners envy," and modern Janeism arguably began with late-colonial nostalgia for a fictional age.

At the end of the nineteenth century, the scholar and critic George Saintsbury coined the term "Janeite," referring to the devotees whom Austen's novels had come to attract or inspire. Borrowing the coinage, Rudyard Kipling published "The Janeites" in 1924, a short story about a band of Brits in World War I who establish a secret brotherhood premised around a cult of Austen. In the story, a lumbering working-class veteran named Humberstall is sweeping the floors of a Masonic lodge in London after the war, where he regales his fellows with recollections of reading Jane at the front. Humberstall is an amiable raconteur but quite clearly shell-shocked, with the "eyes of a bewildered retriever." It was Macklin, Humberstall's "toff" of a commanding officer, who initiated Humberstall into an arcane club of "Janeites"—men who would obsessively reread and circulate the six novels among themselves in the mess halls and the gunneries of their corner of the French front. Warming to Jane, Humberstall says, he consoled himself from the stresses of war by renaming his regiment's three big guns "Mr. Collins," "General Tilney," and "Lady Catherine de Bugg"—a truly wonderful malapropism for "Catherine de Bourgh," the imperious dowager in *Pride & Prejudice*. When Humberstall goes so far as to paint these names on the guns, he is called to a disciplinary tribunal: "They said I was wrong about General Tilney. 'Cordin' to them, our Navy twelve-inch ought to 'ave been christened Miss Bates . . . But they give me full marks for the Reverend Collins—our Nine-point-two."

Why have Kipling's Janeites clung so fiercely, so joyously to Jane? Because it kept them sane, and it kept them alive. "She was the only woman I ever 'eard 'em say a good word for," Humberstall says of his former officers, then quotes Macklin: "It's a very select Society, an' you've got to be a Janeite in your 'eart, or you won't have any success." Upon hearing the account back in London, his fellow Masons express marvel, and jealousy: "No denyin' that Jane business was more useful to you than the Roman Eagles or the Star an' Garter"—honors conferred by Masons among themselves. "Pity there wasn't any of you Janeites in the 'Oly Land. I never come across 'em," laments a veteran of the front against the Turks in Palestine. What Humberstall's new companions envy isn't the reading; it's the fellowship that the reading made possible. "You take it from me, Brethren, there's no one to touch Jane when you're in a tight place," Humberstall says. "Gawd bless 'er, whoever she was." Kipling's story suggests that you don't need to be a "toff," or even educated, to draw pleasure from Austen and the community that she encourages.

•

In 1915, Kipling had gone with his family to Bath, where, in between trips to the pump room, he reread the novels. In a letter from the period, Kipling writes, "The more I read the more I admire and respect and do reverence . . . When she looks straight at a man or a woman she is greater than those who were alive with her—by a whole head . . . with a more delicate hand and a keener scalpel."

His son, John, would die in France later that year, and as Kipling lacerated himself for having been a drumbeater for the war, Austen proved a balm. In a January 1917 diary entry, Mrs. Kipling expresses "delight" at her husband's habit of reading the novels aloud to the family. Here, as so often, Austen's novels functioned as something between entertainment and a kind of moral therapy. If Austen is a keen anatomist of bad fatherhood, a possible prick to Kipling's conscience, she is also the author who brings people together. "I believe Jane was a bit of a matchmaker in a quiet way when she was alive," the narrator of "The Janeites" says. "I know all her books are full of match-making." This remark is confirmed by the Chapman-Metcalfe union, and the many couples who attend Austen conferences together, or who meet one another there—not to mention the platonic affection between Janeites who otherwise would have very little to talk about.

•

Chapman recalled his wartime in Macedonia with a warm nostalgia—he had, after all, survived and returned to his wife—and his reverie of reading Johnson in the high Balkan winds offers a winsome caricature of the solitary scholar:

> I had a camp behind Smol Hill . . . and a six-inch gun (Mark XI, a naval piece, on an improvised carriage; "very rare in this state"), with which I made a demonstration in aid of the French and Greek armies, when they stormed the heights beyond the river; I think in June . . . I had a hut made of sandbags, with a roof constructed of corrugated iron in layers, with large stones between . . . and here, in the long hot afternoons . . . a temporary gunner, in a khaki shirt and shorts, might have been found collating the three editions of the *Tour to the Hebrides*, or re-reading *A Journey to the Western Islands* in the hope of finding a corruption in the text. Ever and again, tiring of collation and emendation, of tepid tea and endless cigarettes, I would go outside to look at the stricken landscape—the parched, yellow hills and ravines, the brown coils of the big snaky river at my feet, the mountains in the blue distance, until the scorching wind, which always blew down that valley, sent me back to the Hebrides.

What's so very important about this passage is how its fancy or ridiculousness fails to dilute—indeed, is bound

up with—its seriousness of purpose: Chapman under-
lines the comical incongruity of a gunner nerding out to
Samuel Johnson in a war zone, even as his lyrical trans-
ports—a sense of privileged dislocation, of being wrested
from the present by the living breath of a previous age—
are entirely earnest, and not unique to Chapman. Editing the text of *Mansfield Park* a few years ago, Claudia
Johnson labored over the placement of a comma until
she had a similar experience to Chapman's: "Again and
again, I read the two sentences aloud quietly to myself to
settle this question until, finally, under these inauspi-
ciously pedantic circumstances, a startling thing happened: I heard Jane Austen breathe."

The point is typographical—a comma indicates,
among other things, where an imagined speaker will take
a breath—but also quite literal: I believe she heard it. Textual recension is an ungrateful task but one of the worthi-
est in the academy, and the thought of Austen animating
that task is irresistible. For two centuries, thousands of
readers have shared such moments of unlikely revelation,
of proximity to Jane or an illusory sense of her presence.
To the more mystical Janeites, that same quiet intake of
breath is our traffic with the ghost of Jane; it is the air
we share when we come together. There is a toast at the
annual JASNA banquet, with hundreds of attendees in
period garb raising their glasses as Austen's likeness is
projected onto various screens around the hall, and the
association's president offers a few words, and there's a

brief pause before any cheers or clinks; slender silence amid so many people is bound to feel holy, and it's in the space of that silence that I first felt the curious presence that Johnson describes.

•

E. M. Forster, one of the more conspicuous Janeites of his age, greeted Chapman's editions with nothing short of rapture. Forster's love for Austen would be lifelong: "I am so fond of her," he said in a BBC broadcast in April 1944. "She's English, I'm English, and my fondness for her may be rather a family affair." He seems to have been particularly roused by the Clarendon editions, and their illuminating notes on the culture of Austen's own time—notes that would prove especially helpful to scholars and admirers of Austen in the States, where such Regency terms as "curricle" and "entail" were not, even in the 1920s, terribly familiar among the general reading public. Chapman's notes were further enlivened by his close attention to, and collation of, Austen's surviving letters, which informed his editing of the novels just as deeply as any Oxonian principles of textual recension. Reviewing Chapman's editions in *The New Republic* in January 1924, Forster told an American audience that the world of Austen worship had been asleep before Chapman, and now it was awake:

I am a Jane Austenite, and, therefore, slightly imbecile about Jane Austen . . . One reads and rereads, the mouth open and the mind closed. Shut up in measureless content, one greets her by the name of most kind hostess, while criticism slumbers. The Jane Austenite possesses none of the brightness he ascribes to his idol . . . For instance, the grammar of the following sentence from *Mansfield Park* presents no difficulty to him: "And, alas! how always known no principle to supply as a duty what the heart was deficient in."

Chapman, in Forster's self-effacing but not unserious account, is one of the few non-imbeciles in the world of Janeites; rather than greeting her "by the name of most kind hostess," Chapman had edited her the way he and his Oxford mentors had edited classical texts in Greek and Latin: the same care and seriousness owed to Lucan was certainly owed to Austen. What a difference it makes, to treat Austen as a serious author! Instead of slumbering, criticism sharpens, and with his faculties intact the critic can pare away lines of dialogue that have run together (Kitty in Chapter II of *Pride & Prejudice*) or restore the sacred placement of a comma, while guiding readers into a fuller version of Austen's world with helpful notes on her family and her age. Forster lavished praise on the utility of Chapman's notes and described Chapman's editing triumph as little short of wizardry: "Without violence, the spell has been broken. The six princesses remain on their sofas, but their eyelids quiver and they move their hands. Their twelve suitors do likewise, and their subordinates stir in the seats to which humor or propriety assigned them."

Then he offers a Janeite's lament:

Yet with all the help in the world, with a fine edition like Mr. Chapman's and the best of literary criticism to our aid, how shall we drag these shy, proud books into the centre of our minds? To be one with Jane Austen! It is a contradiction in terms, yet every Jane Austenite has made the attempt. When the humor has been absorbed and cynicism and moral earnestness both discounted, something remains which is easily called Life, but does not thus become more approachable.

Here, Forster outlines the paradoxes attending this particular area of readerly devotion: books at once shy and proud, and the contradictory impulse to be ourselves and yet to "be one with Jane Austen"—these are peculiarities that pervade the reading of Austen, and persist when we close the book. Needless to say, there is no traditional literary practice that can satisfy a curiosity so singular yet so widespread. "Something remains," Forster says, with a mysteriousness that is not coy; it's the same something that appeared in episodes such as the one Claudia Johnson describes, and that pops briefly into existence whenever Janeites gather.

It is important to emphasize that, were it not for my mother's knees, I might never have entered Austenworld the way I did. Indeed, it took many years of genicular misfortune to land her where she found herself at the time of the *Pride & Prejudice* bicentennial: that is, temporarily crippled and in need of *two* titanium knee replacements within the space of six months.

The knee stuff began when I was very young. We were living in England, and my mother had a nasty habit of falling, especially on cobblestone streets. Mom would trot along, occasionally allowing her toe to scrape the ground, and too often—all the time, in fact—her foot would catch, and down she would plunge. This habit begat a pattern of intensification. The more she fell, the more difficult it was for her to raise her feet above the stones on the street, and the more frequently she would tumble. She made a lot of jokes ("Oh look, I did my tumbling act again; why don't I just join a circus"), but it was awful. I remember Mom in her English-professor uniform, paisley scarves and a nice gray little tweed jacket and those hard black walking heels or else a rugged pair of wood-and-leather clogs, which snagged the cobblestones of London or Oxford or Warwick, until the cycle of occasional tumbles became unbearable. There were lower-back issues, and hand sprains, and, eventually, worse. By 2013, a few months before the camp in Carolina, she needed new knees.

This was no small loss for Austenworld, where my mother has been a semi-regular presence very nearly since the Jane Austen Society of North America began in October 1979 with a group of a hundred Janeites at the Gramercy Park Hotel in Manhattan. And besides worrying me to death, her infirmities would soon send me as a surrogate speaker on her behalf.

•

Allow me to oversimplify. All of Austen is a story about inheritance, from the plays and novellas that she wrote as a teen, to her final compositions, including the last dyspeptic satirical romp of *Sanditon*, a satire on real estate development at an emerging coastal resort. *Pride & Prejudice* is no exception. The novel opens on the five Bennet sisters, who have been born into a fine estate—firmly within the sphere of the gentry—in the countryside of southern England, where they live with their busy and meddling mother and their charming but perilously aloof father. Their comfortable position is threatened only by an unhappy provision in the Bennet will that the estate must pass to a male heir; in this case, the sisters' cousin, an awkwardly unctuous cleric named Collins. Meanwhile, Mr. Darcy, the grand patrician hero, must reconcile his own duties to a far grander estate with his love for the portionless Elizabeth Bennet—alongside his conviction that, despite her hot head and eccentric family, Elizabeth is the one person whose love and wisdom can help him be a better steward. (Darcy is, of course, wildly, inconsolably attracted to her person and her wit—like the mid-twentieth-century critic Lionel Trilling, he can say that "I am meant to fall in love with Lizzy Bennet, and I do.")

But *Pride & Prejudice* is about more subtle modes of inheritance, too, including attitudes and prejudices and a general sense of your role in your neighborhood—in a word, manners. For much of the book, Lizzy emulates her father: from Mr. Bennet, Elizabeth inherits a distrust for affectation, an appetite for reading, a way with an epigram, and a deadpan instinct to enjoy the weaknesses of others. These are qualities that prove powerfully seductive to the reader, who approaches the book through Lizzy's eyes and delights in her persuasive vision of what is what. Throughout the first volume, Austen is so delicate in substituting Lizzy's opinions for your own that you might not notice it until the trick is done.

Yet there is a sinister element to the posture she inherits from her father, who himself seems to alternate between a laughing, Democritean wisdom and something nastier. He mocks their mother right in front of her five daughters and encourages them to do the same; his lack of interest in his youngest daughters prompts him to placate them through innumerable indulgences, and with disastrous consequences.

In the first volume of the novel, Lizzy is as disgusted by Darcy's studious hauteur as she is pleased by her father's ironic distance, and she abjures the one with the same enthusiasm with which she emulates the other. As the book proceeds, though, she recognizes that her father's unremitting archness can be a social liability, while Darcy's supreme emotional continence emerges as something of a virtue: In the novel's first half, Lizzy is her father's daughter, and follows him in deriding her mother's grasping busyness. Only after recognizing how badly her father has mismanaged her younger sisters does Lizzy understand that she's made an error—that she has abrogated practical responsibility in favor of a general superiority. She may have inherited all her father's finest characteristics—his charm, his intelligence—but she also got the bum ones— the intellectual snobbery, the moral arrogance—that, uncorrected, would lead to a life of alienation and sadness.

Again, I am oversimplifying, grossly. The fact remains that Austen's best-known novel is primarily about managing two inheritances: an estate, and a moral sociability. Mr. Rochester attracts Jane Eyre by scowling; Darcy wins Lizzy's love by treating the servants kindly.

This is one reason that I am unmoved by readers who throw down the book and say it's all just so much marriage plot. To quote *Clueless*: As if! Marriage is merely the capstone, the emblem that marks a moment of larger social renewal. The real business of the novel is not arranging the wedding—it's about arranging a community such that it is ready to celebrate and be enriched by the new couple. There is something unbearably selfish about the two-person romance, about Romeo and Juliet or Heathcliff and Catherine. Austen's novels do not belong to this species of love story. They are ensemble affairs, not duos against the world, and they're far more concerned with the question of how to live among our fellow beings than how to marry your best friend. The books end in weddings, but that doesn't make them love stories—it just makes them comedies.

An iconic scene in *Pride & Prejudice* finds Lizzy in a copse of trees, reading a letter from Darcy that unravels nearly all of her prior beliefs about his conduct and character. At last, with a sort of awful clarity, she speaks aloud—"How despicably I have acted! . . . Till this moment, I never knew myself." Certain contemporary readers accustomed to the rhythms of romantic comedy read this moment as the end of self-denial, the moment when Lizzy owns that, yes, she does have the hots for Darcy. Such readers miss the point entirely. Elizabeth has indeed arrived at revelation, but it's nothing as silly or as selfish as shouting her love from the mountaintop; it's a serious moment of self-censure for having misread nearly every social cue that she's received throughout the book, and for having harmed those she loves as a result. This is not the self-seeking of intimate love; it's the self-censure of a social conscience.

I've come to think of this as the right way to understand why Austen is so particularly suited to a crossover conference that feels a bit more like a camp or festival. Austen makes a great deal of sense as a unifying pop figure who can bring together so many people. Her novels don't offer us solitary rhapsodies so much as social possibilities, and Janeites don't wander aimlessly but navigate together, tacking and then correcting, like any good Austen heroine, when we recognize that our path is askew, or that we're bound for a collision. The arrangements for the conference mirrored the proceedings of a gentry house party from 1813 or 1793, with grad students playing the precocious children and younger set who provide the central energy and occasional scandal—and also stage a racy play, much as Austen's family had done and the young Bertrams do in *Mansfield Park*; the professors were the parents, clergymen, and aunts, alternately making matches and decrees; the civilians became the neighborhood—Meryton or Highbury or so on—and the finely drawn secondary characters who reflect us back to ourselves. In Austenworld, even our roles—our *duties*—can feel inherited from the world of Jane.

In the weeks ahead of the summer camp, I had tried to anticipate the scene, the dramatis personae, but imagination failed. I knew the novels, and much of Austen's biography, but this scene of modern-day fanatics would be, to me, entirely new. Concerned friends were far more vivid in their forecasts. Upon hearing that I'd be nestled among the Janeites, one friend expressed alarm and another deep jealousy. Many who wrote me in advance of that first summer camp shared clear prejudices about Janeites. They seemed to think that anyone who went to these things would have to be insufferably pretentious, or insufferably boring, or both, or else pathetically unhappy in love and resigned to a life of cat-fancying and book clubs; joyless people without imagination; readers who long for the manners of a lost age because they can't hack it in their own. This is all massively silly. You can level many accusations at someone willing to render themselves ludicrous by tripping on their evening gown or busting a button on their corset, but being "boring" isn't among them. Anyone who cannot find entertainment and variety at an Austen conference is more to be pitied than censured, but there's no reason we can't do both. A lot of this widespread reaction is very clearly gendered—a requisite posture of disdain from all men from puberty onward. It would be an insufferable knitting circle, one buddy said; an old editor told me I would grow so sick of the Austen world I'd never read the novels again—or else (he mused) I'd find myself brainwashed and never read anything else; it would be a great place to pick up chicks; it would be a terrible place to pick up chicks, et cetera. Of course, everyone was wrong.

I had now caught my first glimpse of the Janeites. Soon I would see them in their private ecstasies and public rhapsodies: the secret love they steal in chaste kisses at the ball; the versions of Austen that they write and rewrite, adding sex or switching gender or extending the narrative beyond the happily drawn conclusions whose very artifice is so often a joke for Austen.

The closest comparison is to a religious diaspora, a far-flung church, whose functionaries convene in heterodox worship—the group comes together over shared enthusiasm for its primum mobile, and at the same time, once together, comports itself (as best it can) by the letter of the text as handed down through Chapman and Metcalfe and Johnson and the rest. I do not mean to overstate, nor to mock, nor to imply immodest zeal among these good people. Janeism is a religion only in these two respects—reverence for the Godhead, and adherence to the text.

•

Friday morning saw ninety degrees before breakfast, and as I approached the brick eminence of Hyde Hall, with its octagonal faux-gatehouse and happy little cloistered gardens, an older woman eyed my nametag and green lanyard, the greenness of which indicated that I was an "organizer." She waved me down with a retractable umbrella.

"Young man," she observed, by way of summons. I smiled and squinted over my sunglasses.

"Milady."

"I do not know what is happening."

"Yes?"

"I wish to attend the plenary panel on 'Austen and Romance.'"

"It's right inside," I said, pointing toward the French windows of Pemberley. "You can't miss it."

The lady shook her head. "But then I'm to proceed to Rosings, and I am confused." She thrust her schedule of events in my direction.

"The two venues are awfully close, and both inside. I'm happy to show you, if you like."

"I don't see how we can remember all these rooms," she said with a stare, as though I were guilty of some architectural misdemeanor. "Longbourne looks quite as nice as the others, and really it shouldn't. Do you agree?"

"I do see your point. But then, Hunsford or the Cheapside house wouldn't quite have the same ring, you know?"

She paused for a moment. "But what will you do for *Sense & Sensibility*?" she asked. "How will you keep all the rooms straight?"

I laughed. "Well, that's getting a year ahead of ourselves. Of course, we could hold a session on 'the picturesque,' but we'd have to find the right moor, and probably a fog machine as well."

She appraised me again without smiling. "I am off for tea. We can conclude our discussion in Pemberley, if you like."

"It would give me pleasure."

I disengaged myself, wolfed two plates of fruit in the Hyde kitchen, donned and straightened my blazer, and made for the panelists' table at Pemberley, there to chair the plenary on "Austen and Romance." Inger had provided laminated cue cards, with which I was to signal each scholar when her time was winding down. The first said FIVE MINUTES LEFT; the final, YOU'VE DELIGHTED US LONG ENOUGH. Though it was a supposedly simple task, the enthusiasm of the speakers often dwarfed my modest efforts, and the cue cards, masterful bits of passive-aggressiveness as they were, proved less useful than, say, a shepherd's crook, which would have been more direct.

One of the panelists began to quote the first line of *Pride & Prejudice*—"It is a truth universally acknowl-edged, that a single man in possession of a good fortune, must be in want of a wife"—and by "acknowledged" the full audience had joined in. Seventy-plus adults intoning this sentence is wonderful and creepy in equal measure; think the Nicene Creed, delivered by ebullient zombies.

TWO

Dressing the Part

So the secret got out, and still delights each new participant.

—R. W. Chapman, introduction to Jane Austen's letters

Young men first starting out in life will often ask me how to land a regular gig playing Mr. Darcy. The procedure, I tell them (for I am generous with my counsel), is as follows. First, ensure a partial upbringing in England. It is desirable also that you will have spent your tween years falling in love with Jennifer Ehle's Elizabeth Bennet in Andrew Davies's 1995 BBC adaptation of *Pride & Prejudice*. But I also explain that the single most important element in becoming Mr. Darcy is simply to be the only male in a graduate seminar on the novels of Jane Austen. If you're a guy in that scenario, and people start talking about dress-up, it won't be long before someone squeezes you into tights and pushes you out in front of the crowd, enjoining you with a wink to "take one for the team."

If you're at a ball, and a lady asks you to dance, oblige, even though Darcy might have done otherwise. If you are not dancing and you spot a lady looking demure and unspoken-for at the fringe of the dance, ask her for the honor of a turn about the room. Shyness is nearly as bad as conceit in a Darcy reenactor—either can prevent you from swinging a leg on the dance floor.

A final piece of advice to young would-be Darcys— and this is far from trivial—is to identify and ingratiate yourself with some good dependable people in the Theater Department of the closest university. These are the people whose wisdom, and whose sewing machines, will see you and your six-piece costume through even the hottest summer conference—indeed, my costumer friends were soon serving in a sort of double capacity, offering spiritual support as well as roadside assistance; they bucked my spirit while mending my front-flap Regency breeches.

The Janeites are famous for many things, but perhaps none so much as a delight in wearing the garb—the Empire-waist dresses, the cravats, the buckle shoes that squeak on a polished floor while you're dancing to the "Duke of Kent's Waltz." You can call this dress-up, or make-believe, or adults behaving like children. The widely preferred term in the twenty-first century is "cosplay," a modish portmanteau of "costume" and "play" that still, even after so many conferences and balls and Cornish teas, strikes a racy note in my imagination. The term is expansive and applies to people attending *Star Trek* conventions or KISS concerts or Renaissance fairs or Civil War reenactments, but also to various demi-mondes of sexual role-play.

A young man always remembers his first Darcy outfit.

•

When I agreed to help organize the summer camp, I anticipated that the duties would be mainly clerical. I was not entirely wrong—there was no shortage of bureaucracy to administer, whether it meant collating Thursday's dinner orders or apportioning space for the costumers or introducing the scholarly panels or striving against hope to persuade those panels to end. The grad students were scurrying around like servants at the inauguration of a country house party. But there were more flamboyant duties, too. The big news dropped on me one morning about a month before the camp in a warm but firm e-mail from Inger, informing me that I would need to be fitted for Regency breeches.

"The committee has decided that we need a Mr. Darcy at the ball," she wrote, before indicating that Adam would play Mr. Bingley and Ashley would play his sister. The e-mail concluded with a request that felt more like a fiat: "Will you be our Mr. Darcy?" The brain trust promised to provide a six-piece costume and was quite insistent that I shave my beard. Somehow the beard was the least of my concerns. Taking on the role of Mr. Darcy involves a lot of pressure, since any pretender is liable to suffer by comparison with the dreamy gents who have played the role in the past—foremost among them Colin Firth, whose rendition of the patrician hero is the high-water mark for civilized sexiness. This latter concern felt very real; while I have great faith in my posture and bearing and general manners, I have never labored under the delusion that I am a matinee idol. Simply to accept the role might smack of arrogance, I feared—"What, *Ted* thinks he's sufficiently dashing to play Mr. Darcy?!" But declining, even politely, would be worse; no better, indeed, than Darcy's own behavior at the Meryton Assembly, where he famously and unforgivably abstains from dancing "when gentlemen were scarce and more than one young lady was sitting down in want of a partner." I had even been planning in secret to slip away from the ball early on Saturday night. Some men might have taken the e-mail as cause for vanity; I took it as cause for brief anxiety.

But there was little room for refusal, and the following week I found myself on the second floor of the Carolina Performing Arts Center, where a professor named Jade tried to make me look elegant. Jade herself is a picture of elegance—she wore her hair semi-short in a sort of stylish neo-pompadour over an arch pair of tortoise-shell spectacles that would rise a bit on her nose whenever she smiled. Given my mechanical cluelessness in the face of these foreign raiments, she had cause to smile frequently.

"Adam gets off a bit easier," she explained as she arrayed the six pieces of the suit before me. We were in a dressing room down the hall from Jade's office, surrounded by bonnets and muslins of various colors and some shiny, leathery numbers that felt out of place—more futuristic than retrospective. A pair of fake swords reclined against a mirror. "He's wearing a black outfit, very clergyman, a bit less flashy." Jade indicated the suit in question. She was right. It looked beyond clerical—the sort of outfit that Mr. Collins might have rejected as too stuffy. Mine, Jade warned me as I pulled on the flowy white shirt, would be rather more flamboyant.

But first, the tights. Of the many kindnesses I have experienced in Austenworld, few matched the depth of generous patience with which Jade waited while I plunged one leg after the other into the tights that she had selected for me. This was not reticence on my part, and certainly not discomfort at what felt like close proximity to drag. It was a much simpler clumsiness that made me feel oddly emasculated.

"You know, I used to be better at this," I said after a moment, through the partition that Jade, in her regard for my modesty, had placed between us in the dressing room. It was true; my sophomore year in high school, I had appeared as Puck in a production of *A Midsummer Night's Dream*, during which I set several speed records slipping into a skintight costume. That verve and confidence of my younger self now felt very far away.

Jade dealt gently with my incompetence: "Are there . . . any questions I can answer?"

I acknowledged that, like Scrooge on Christmas morning, I had made "a perfect Laocoön" of myself with these stockings—that is to say, I had become tangled in my tights.

"Have you watched women put on tights?"

It felt like a loaded question. "Sure," I said. "I mean, I grew up around women, and they were often putting on tights."

"Do you remember how they did it?"

A pause. Duh. "They bunch them together and stick their foot in and then they sort of . . . never mind, I got this." I bunched the tights, inserted my feet, and rolled the fabric up my legs, in imitation of the women in my life, regretting in silence that I had worn boxer shorts, which never fit well under tights. The effect was even snugger than I had anticipated but not entirely disagreeable. The silk integument of the tights offered a pleasant sense of support; the unfamiliar stricture gave me a feeling of powerful security. Jade handed me the breeches, then glided off to grab the centerpiece of the costume: *the blue topcoat*.

"This is really something" is how she prepared me for the thing. It was a middle-weight wool affair that would qualify as "slim fit" by today's standards, its stiff half-collar protruding above the broad-shouldered cut, taper-

ing down to hug the waist; the train of the coat fell roughly
to my knees, but the front ended just below the waistcoat,
the better to display the handsome stitching of the vest
and the imposing front flap of the cream-colored breeches.
The style, I heard Jade explain (while I stared, smitten, at
the coat), was "cutaway," just like in the movies, and I
had to admire the cumulative effect of the costume into
which she had inserted me with such kindness and care.
Jade angled me toward the dressing-room mirror.

"Ted, meet Mr. Darcy," she said.

•

The next time I tried on the outfit, it felt more comfortable. I was in my house and had just rolled the tights onto
my legs when my housemate, Jerrod, came through the
door. Our eyes met for a moment, in silence.

"So you're really going for this Jane Austen thing," he
observed, deadpan.

I must have been a spectacle—poufy shirt dangling to
my waist, where a pair of cream-colored tights encased
my boxer shorts. Jerrod is a scholar of Edmund Spenser
whose ambitious dissertation concerned early Semitic lan-
guages, but he is also at heart an unaffected man, who
grew up as a hunter in Lorain, Ohio, and whose first jobs
were all commercial fishing gigs on Lake Erie.

"Laugh all you want," I said, and Jerrod obliged. But
he also helped me with the double-hook that fastened
the pre-tied cravat to my poufy shirt, and stood to the side
while I tightened the waistcoat and popped on the blue

topcoat. I drew myself up in front of the mirror, arched an eyebrow, and tried to scowl.

My own slender face stared back at me, and for a moment the effect was complete—I felt dislocated. Who was this in the looking glass? A long-lost ancestor. A caricature of a Janeite. A twentysomething punk who had decided to dress as Mr. Darcy for Halloween. I was peering at myself, but not. It was hard not to laugh. The blue topcoat felt both foolishly elegant and totally rock 'n' roll. I could have been dressing as Darcy or as Prince.

"You should send a pic to your mom," Jerrod said. When I did, she called. By this time I had warmed to the costume and was making faces into the mirror.

"I just got the photo," she said, and I could hear her smiling because she sounded a little singsongy on the word "just." I bowed to the mirror and mugged a face of deep seriousness before grinning like a toddler.

"Isn't this outfit just—" I had no adjective, and Mom cut me off.

"You're wearing that to the ball, right?"

"Yes, Mom."

"James says it will be a majestic ball on the Saturday night."

"Yes, Mom."

"You know there will be a shortage of men." She meant that I would have to dance. I weighed duty against some wordless aversion to the idea.

"You realize they're not paying me nearly enough for all this."

"I want you to make a good impression," she said flatly. "It would mean so much to everyone there." (Mothers are masters of projecting their prejudices onto the world.) I didn't say anything, though some part of me knew I wouldn't disobey. She pressed her point home: "Please don't fight me on this."

I told her I would probably dance.

"Please don't say 'probably.'"

I felt we had wandered from the main subject, which was the awesomeness of my Darcy outfit.

"Isn't the vest just amazing?"

"It's a waistcoat," Mom sighed. "Pronounced '*west-*kit.' Don't say 'vest.' *Please* don't say 'vest' during the conference."

"Yes, Mom." I pulled a Michael Jackson kick in front of the mirror, then tried and failed to moonwalk.

•

The "shortage of men" problem is a very real one at Austen gatherings. If you're younger than sixty and a male, you'll sometimes look up during a scholarly panel or a session of dance instruction or the Saturday tea and begin to worry that your fellow men have all perished in some far-off place. As the summer camp progressed, I began to feel more and more like an exotic creature, a man who through luck or connections has avoided the Napoleonic Wars and thereby become something of a hot commodity on the home front. By the second day, women my mother's age were asking (with varying degrees of coquetry) whether I would save a dance for them. I would come to learn that this was the curious reception I could expect at any Austen event. At my first visit to JASNA, in Minneapolis three months later, a woman ushered her seventeen-year-old daughter toward me, calling me "the answer to a prayer." At the following year's JASNA meeting in Montréal, a woman dressed as Lady Catherine de Bourgh clasped my wrist at the ball and asked: "Where on earth did you come from?" It's a lot of fun but also a lot of pressure.

I do not wish to exaggerate. Dressing as Mr. Darcy at an Austen symposium is like playing Mickey Mouse at Disney World. I have now been to several major Austen conferences in the United States and Canada, wearing a modified version of the Darcy suit at each, and each time the effect was the same. And its effect on me was equally silly, and equally wonderful: I became quieter and some-what gentler in my manners, and felt at the same time that I was an inch or two taller (the cutaway topcoat with tight shoulders basically requires immaculate posture). And this is the funny part of Austen cosplay—how un-silly it all feels: the escapist element is bound up with the element of discovery, and the costume allows you for a brief and hallowed moment to enter a new version of yourself. Any-one who has ever worn a tuxedo to a prom or a black suit to a funeral will understand some measure of what I'm describing—and the more elaborate or outré the costume, the more we feel a sense of regression to some earlier phase of life, when we celebrated pajama day in first grade and dressed as Groucho Marx for Halloween.

But playacting as a twentysomething offers pleasures other than those of childhood. If the wordless enthusiasms of childhood dress-up have calmed with age, the costume has not lost its transportive quality. The right hat can induce gentility; in a fine cravat and topcoat, you wouldn't think twice about lending your chaise-and-four to a beautiful young lady with a case of the sniffles. It's not just about looks or some idealized reflection of yourself, though it is perhaps easiest to idealize oneself in a world unbound from time. The simple feel of the clothes, the grip of the starch, the Speedo-grade rectitude of the shoulders, not to mention the taut garments that support the body's nether constituents—each of these elements will change your bearing from the outset, assuming you've been properly fitted. The point here isn't that a high collar elevates your thinking, exactly. If Goethe tells us that "to speak another language is to possess another soul," then donning a costume means adjusting your shoulders to the posture of another era. After I had tried on the outfit, I compared notes with Adam, asking him whether he felt at all different. He laughed.

"The impression," he said, "was instant."

•

The weekend of the summer camp proved my awakening to the world of Austen-mania, but not until later that year, when I attended the big annual meeting of JASNA—again as a surrogate for my mother—did I begin to recognize the full scope of this frenzied love, the full varieties of this fandom. JASNA is simply huge; its official members number more than five thousand, and each year, attendance at the annual general meeting numbers several hundred at least, and more in anniversary years—sometimes limited only by local fire codes. Attending JASNA in any year is a sort of hajj for Janeites; its sprawling membership is the empire in which our own modest Austen summer camp counted as a very minor province.

There is no richer survey of American enthusiasm for Jane Austen than the public market at the Jane Austen Society of North America. JASNA's market is usually a converted meeting room or business center on the third floor of whatever upscale hotel is hosting the annual conference, the sort of cavernous carpeted space that comprises anywhere between two and six rooms, demarcated by discreet accordion-dividers and generally reserved for sales conferences, corporate team-building activities, and prix fixe New Year's dinners for discerning couples.

When JASNA comes to town, the scene slips back two centuries. Miss Lisa Brown, proprietress of Regency Rentals, peddles her costumes ("Ladies Sizes 2–26; Gentlemen Sizes 36–52 [chest]") and will corner you to point out an errant kerchief or an imperfection in a waistcoat, which she assures you she can restore with minimal damage to your pocketbook. Syrie James will pause from hawking the evening's theatrical adaptation to press into your hands a copy of her novel *Jane Austen's First Love*, a fictional account of Austen's summer flirtation with Edward Taylor, upon whom (the Austen letters indicate) Austen had "fondly doted." Women and men dressed as period haberdashers will remain in character while pressing homemade bonnets upon you; other people dressed as period haberdashers do not remain in character but nonetheless press homemade bonnets upon you.

Outside the market, authors perch behind a row of tables, selling and signing books and answering questions from their public. At one table, several of the world's most decorated Austen scholars share sympathy over their colleagues' physical ailments while fielding breathless questions from graduate students for whom the presence of these scholars has the effect of an oracular experience. Four tables to their right, another author is peddling romantic spin-offs of the Austen novels—there is even a subset of fanfiction predicated on subtextual homoeroticism in the original books; you wouldn't believe what Darcy and Bingley get up to when the rest of Netherfield is asleep—and, to her right, two authors are signing mystery novels (*The Suspicion at Sanditon!*). If you poked your head in from the street, you might meet Devoney Looser, a professor at Arizona State University and an accomplished roller-derbyist who, when she's on skates, goes by the moniker "Stone Cold Jane Austen." Depending on the year, you might bump into John Mullan, a perceptive critic of Austen who has also answered one of the enduring questions of Austenworld: How many umbrellas appear in the novels? How many of them are furled? (The answers are seven and six, respectively.)

If you're especially lucky, you will meet Julia Matson and her collection of "Bingley's Teas," a line of globally sourced, exquisitely flavorful infusions and leaf concoctions that could make a tea-obsessive of even the most American reader; her blends are often named for the Austen character whom each evokes. "Lydia Has More Fun," for example, is a caffeine-free tisane that tastes "flirty, flaky, without the usual substance of common sense," while "Mr. Darcy's Pride" is an "elegant and dark" oolong with "a bold beginning yet a smooth finish." On special occasions, Julia surprises her favorite customers with secret packets of Lapsang souchong in the mail, while at conferences, she dispenses samples before a mischievous poster of a very arch-looking Frenchwoman in an Empire-waist frock with a strap hanging boldly off one shoulder. The only text on the poster is in a large, stylish font: "Jane Austen was a loose woman too."

Julia has been scolded for this poster on more than one occasion—I'm assuming mainly by people who don't get the wordplay with "loose tea," which is what Julia sells. The year I met her, at a meeting in Montréal, a woman dressed her down in a manner worthy of Lady Catherine de Bourgh upbraiding a slovenly seamstress. The woman's argument, as best I can recall, was that Austen was *not* a loose woman and indeed would *never* have worn such a frock, and that commodifying Dear Jane into a sex kitten merely to sell high-end tea constituted an assault of the highest order. We were unable to confirm whether this firebrand critic had leveled similar censure toward the erotica peddlers who sat just a few tables away.

"It is remarkable," Julia wrote me, toward the end of a long and hilarious string of text messages in which we rehashed this encounter, "that there exist Janeites who possess absolutely no sense of humor."

Julia is right to consider such a reaction remarkable— the poster is essentially PG—yet the battle over who Austen was, what she would approve, and, yes, even what she would wear, has been raging for ages. While priggish Janeites (I have found) are relatively rare in the contemporary world, their lineage is long and august. This mode of hagiography began essentially as soon as Austen died in 1817. That same year, her brother Henry prefaced the posthumous release of *Persuasion* and *Northanger Abbey* with a decorous "Biographical Notice" that described Austen's life in pious terms, one of "usefulness, literature, and religion." We learn, too, that Austen enjoyed Samuel Johnson's moral writings and admired Samuel Richardson's command of character, while distrusting Henry Fielding, in whom "neither nature, wit, nor humour, could make her amends for so very low a scale of morals." This little bio of Henry's reads as a tacit family disavowal of any potentially subversive elements in the novels—a strange and sanitizing beatification, like the addled panegyrics that Roman poets used to write upon the death, and alleged apotheosis, of murderous emperors.

Henry's biographical notice struck at least one seg-
ment of his sister's audience as narrow and uptight, and
before long, the earliest generation of Janeites was rebel-
ling against this sterile and unsatisfactory account of the
novelist. In 1821, the *Englishwoman's Domestic Magazine*
responded to the ongoing beatification of Austen in a col-
umn of Austenian verve:

> We have never read of such perfection elsewhere
> except in epitaphs, and though we know that *de
> mortuis nil nisi bonum* should be uttered, we confess
> we wish her biographer had recorded some fault,
> and if not exactly a fault, a failing, a weakness, a
> peccadillo of the most frivolous character, such as
> daintiness in eating, or nervous fidgeting, for then
> we might have pictured her as a mortal woman,
> with a coalscuttle bonnet, sandaled shoes, and
> mittens of the period, but now we can think of her
> as nothing less than an angel writing novels with a
> quill plucked from one of her own wings, and un-
> fortunately there is no known likeness of her to dis-
> sipate the idea.

Of course, the modern Janeite now has access to at
least one likeness of the novelist, though this is hardly
better than none; in the miniature watercolor sketch, at-
tributed to her sister, Cassandra, Austen's features appear sharp and slightly pinched but pretty and not

inelegant; the family apparently agreed that it was un-flattering. When Jane's nephew James Edward Austen-Leigh published his *Memoir of Jane Austen* in 1870, the publishers commissioned an engraving based on Cassandra's sketch; examining the engraving, James's younger sister Caroline said: "There is a *look* which I recognize as *hers* . . . though the general resemblance is not strong." As Claudia Johnson writes: "The image gives a characteristically paradoxical impression of being at once definite and faint, solid and imminently evaporable." The modern reader, then, has only a weak idea of her resemblance, and Janeites in general are content to accept the Cassandra miniature as a sort of coloring-book cutout or paper doll, which we can shade and texture and dress however we like.

It is important, I think, that the editors of the *Englishwoman's Domestic Magazine* should focus so closely (and virtuosically) on clothes in this passage, and I love the idea that Austen's mortality is somehow contained in her coalscuttle bonnet—the notion that a simple swatch of her clothing could tell us more than Henry's whole memoir. This was 1821; just four years after her death, Austen had entered the popular imagination as a formidable and vanished genius, whom you could recover if only you knew the cut of her frock. I don't blame the editors for this reaction; it is a cold, pious, almost unfeeling Jane with whom we're presented in her brother's memoir, a figure that hardly squares with the light and liveliness of the novels.

Purity and saintliness are found only in abstraction; imperfection and character are found in particulars. Much like modern Janeites, many of Austen's earlier readers wanted to see past the saint, and to know *all* the particulars. They—*we*—want to know the cut of the dress. And we definitely want to know the ratio of furled to unfurled umbrellas in the novels.

Still, throughout the Victorian and Edwardian periods, Austen was installed in the pantheon of English letters both as a sort of mannequin for English virtue—a moral-didactic paragon—and as the laureate of a lost age of English order and excellence, who offered a languorous vision of nostalgia that Brits, weary from war, could slip into like a warm bath. By the mid-nineteenth century, English and American pilgrims were earnestly processing from Boston or Birmingham to visit Austen's grave at Winchester, and after J. E. Austen-Leigh published his *Memoir* in 1870, the number and frequency of these pilgrimages only increased. "Jane lies in Winchester / Blessèd be her shade," as Kipling writes in the epitaph quatrain that serves as prelude to "The Janeites," and I have a hard time believing that the echo of the Lord's Prayer is accidental. Kipling's grenadiers, of course, are not of the escapist class—they are firmly lower- and working-class—but Kipling's verse lines remind us of the bourgeois atmosphere of retrospective worship that attended Austen between 1870 and the Second World War.

This priggish view of Austen prevailed until the 1930s

and '40s, and one of the most important turns came not from Forster or Chapman but from a psychologist named D. W. Harding. In 1940, Harding pilloried Austen's more humorless worshippers in an essay called "Regulated Hatred: An Aspect of the Work of Jane Austen," in which he observes that Austen's "books are, as she meant them to be, read and enjoyed by precisely the sort of people whom she disliked." This is the sort of line that should give any conscientious Janeite pause. In Harding's view, the idea of Austen as a model of virtue and a preserver of national character was a thin piety that erased (or sought to erase) the more corrosive or critical elements in the novels, all while disclaiming their author's sense of vital, vicious fun. Such pieties are inimical to a full and proper enjoyment of Austen, and Harding wanted to recapture her from the stuffy moralists and the middle-brow worshippers. He would rather have Austen read by "those who would turn to her not for relief and escape but as a formidable ally against things and people which were to her, and still are, hateful." Harding's argument is at heart anti-Janeite—he rails against the supposedly soft, acritical stance of fandom, while also suggesting that Austen studies had been too feminized, too much about pleasure and identification and not enough about manly, analytical rigor. Still, he makes a good point. If all you're seeking is a saint to comfort you, Harding argues, you'll miss the ambivalences, the really difficult and rewarding contradictions of the novels. "Pictures of perfection, as you know, make me sick and wicked," Austen once wrote in a letter to her sister. Yet we're still making those pictures and still chastising those whose pictures of Austen are otherwise.

Like Julia, Harding finds remarkable the irony that there are Janeites who seem to have no sense of irony about themselves, no apparent glee for mischief, no inner Lizzy Bennet.

Each generation has always dressed Austen as it saw fit—indeed, within each generation, the individual reader will always fashion Jane depending on the way we first encounter her, and on our own particular prejudices. Part of being a fan means recognizing that Austen belongs equally to all of us, even as we feel viscerally that everyone else has got her utterly wrong. Like all fans, we are by necessity irrational creatures. It is lovely to have one's enthusiasms endorsed, and the more arcane the enthusiasm, the more welcome the endorsement. Still, Janeites would not be Janeites without squabbles over the text and how to interpret the Word, so factions inevitably appear: one visiting Janeite will insist on Austen's youthful Jacobitic conservatism, or else play up the protofeminist subversion most pronounced in the *Juvenilia* and perhaps her final, unfinished novel. One visitor will stress Austen's late-life conversion to English Evangelism, and another will counter that Austen was a quiet Anglican who could address adultery without sermonizing. One bloc will call her a shy, retiring maiden-aunt, while others will say (much more the vogue these days) that Austen was a woman whose perspective, if not her itinerary, was cosmopolitan, formed by reading international newspapers and receiving detailed letters from two globe-navigating sailor-brothers. Seth Grahame-Smith has reimagined her, lucratively, as a zombie slayer; Julia has reimagined her, archly, as a "loose woman."

This mode of correctivist biographical criticism is not, of course, unique to Austen scholarship, but our fashioning of Austen always seems to involve higher stakes, or at least a more passionate audience, than it does with other authors. A professor of mine once noted, "You don't see bumper stickers that say: 'I'd rather be reading Tolstoy.'" The annual Jane Austen Festival in Louisville, Kentucky, features a shirtless, bare-knuckle boxing match—the sort of country entertainment that was popular in Austen's day. Spectators are dressed, without fail, in full Regency regalia. As a vulgar Janeite once whispered to me, during a particularly spirited Janeite parade in Montréal: *Where else on earth could you see this shit?* The answer is, nowhere—not even at a Byron conference.

Possessiveness over our picture of Jane has always been part of our inheritance as fans. Writing about the Chapman editions of the novels in *The New Republic* in 1924, Virgina Woolf complained: "There are 25 elderly gentlemen living in the neighborhood of London who resent any slight upon her genius as if it were an insult offered to the chastity of their aunts." Julia and I consoled ourselves with this bracing, evergreen truth while we gossiped about the woman who had taken such exception to her "loose woman" poster. We agreed that Jane's brother Henry had his revenge after all, in those few remaining Janeites who feel a righteous fury when they see a portrait of Austen in a come-hither dress—who resent any cosmetic slight against their picture of perfection.

The graduate students and a majority of the civilians attended our first round of dance instruction on Friday in Gerrard Hall, a great two-story oblong building, seemingly designed for the elegant length of a Regency cotillion. The balcony, which runs along three walls, is an ideal viewing gallery, and several of the children had already staked their claim to the most desirable seats. Jack Maus, a deadpan instructor supplied by the Regency Assembly of North Carolina, led us through such dances as the "Physical Snob" (perhaps my favorite) and the "Duke of Kent's Waltz," which Maus described as "not a waltz at all because you're not allowed to touch!" Maus is an old hand at this sort of thing—there is significant demand for his brand of instruction, and academic Austen gatherings constitute a minority of his business; far more frequent are book-club galas and seasonal cotillions for historically minded hobbyists. Like so many of the weekend's visitors, he is a fixture in the great year-round cycle of

Regency cosplay and general Austen worship that often remains invisible to the uninitiated.

Throughout the hour-long workshop, Maus's directives were no-nonsense, stentorian. "This will be much simpler if I am the only one talking," he would say into his body mic, and also: "Please, my good people, *stop dancing*. Listen. Watch."

One or two ladies spoke under their breath about what Maus could do with his directives, but largely we were an obedient flock, and Maus shepherded us through "Mr. Beveridge's Maggot" and one or two other numbers until we could reproduce them in tolerable fashion, if not with utter grace. The younger generation (I include the graduate students here) seemed more comfortable on the twirling, kaleidoscopic dances; the stationary foot maneuvers required to "set" in most dances proved far more befuddling. For those of us wearing our costumes, whether in whole or in part, there were added layers of distraction.

Many of the die-hard attendees quickly mastered their moves, and I began to feel like the worst kind of impostor. I consoled myself afterward by staging tableaux with Ashley, now wearing her Caroline Bingley outfit, which was in fact the wedding dress in which she'd just been married. We amused ourselves for fifteen minutes taking photographs of each other and eventually arrayed Ashley across two or three chairs to effect a sort of time-lapse swoon. In the penultimate shot, she fans herself as a dire expression clouds her features. In the final shot, Caroline

Bingley is suddenly operating an iPhone, texting with her husband, transported from 1813 back to the present and, by tenuous satellite connection, to a unit in the Middle East. "I'm so sorry, Caroline Bingley should know to put her phone on vibrate."

I told her that was silly, and that she should talk to her husband, but the sense of dislocation was strong, and my own phone suddenly felt very foreign in my hand.

A tiny child bounced past us outside Gerrard, repeating: "We shall see you at the ball! We shall see you at the ball!" The silent auction had begun. "The winners will be announced tomorrow evening after the harpist has finished playing," Inger said, as though announcing the time. Ashley rose from her swoon to accompany me in the direction of Pemberley, where further time-travel preparations awaited us.

There's a major irony to these Austen gatherings, and it's not merely D. W. Harding's indelible burn against Janeites—that the mass of us represent "precisely the sort of people whom [Austen] disliked." The irony is the idea that it's useful, virtuous, or even acceptable to dress like your favorite literary characters. The costumes are at the center of the lettered enthusiasm that drives Janeites toward one another, but Austen herself had expressed specific distaste for this very sort of literary emulation.

The passage I'm thinking of appears in a pair of letters that Austen wrote to her sister, Cassandra, in 1796. In the first, dated January 9, Jane tells Cassandra that she has been flirting with a young man, her "Irish friend," a distant cousin named Tom Lefroy. It is one of the classics of morning-after literature:

> You scold me so much in the nice long letter which I have this moment received from you, that I am almost afraid to tell you how my Irish friend and I behaved. Imagine to yourself everything most profligate and shocking in the way of dancing and sitting down together. I can expose myself however, only once more, because he leaves the country soon after next Friday, on which day we are to have a dance at Ashe after all. He is a very gentlemanlike, good-looking, pleasant young man, I assure you. But as to our having ever met, except at the three last balls, I cannot say much; for he is so excessively laughed at about me at Ashe, that he is ashamed of coming to Steventon, and ran away when we called on Mrs. Lefroy a few days ago.

The playacting here is lovely—when Austen writes about flirtation, her style inevitably becomes lighter and more teasing—and the technique of this letter, like so many of the others, shows us a lot about how Austen went about creating fiction. (She was twenty when she wrote this and had just completed a revision of *Pride & Prejudice*.) Even in corresponding with her sister, Austen is panoramic and psychological; she captures the competing attitudes of the room and casts herself and her admirer through the eyes of the onlookers—their quite-conventional behavior (dancing and talking) assumes the proportions of a neighborhood scandal, worthy of the first volume in any of her novels. Austen's letters are full of similar social tableaux, and their double charm is that behind the arch front that her style presents lies an earnest truth. Even as she performs a sort of mock-mortification, she betrays a very real enthusiasm, for the ball and for the young man. It's small wonder that Chapman claimed to reread the letters for pleasure. Once you've exhausted the novels and the *Juvenilia*, a true Janeite will find that the letters are nearly as reliable in their delights.

Lefroy soon left the neighborhood—he would eventually become chief justice of Ireland—and we might never know whether he left a chink in Austen's heart or not, but certainly she sounds a little down on the day of his departure: "At length the day is come on which I am to flirt my last with Tom Lefroy, and when you receive this it will be over. My tears flow as I write at the melancholy idea." I've always read this passage as archness posing as ambivalence: the tears I take to be real but I also sense a colder element at play, the suggestion that Austen will miss the flirting more than she'll miss the boy. There will be many people (more than you realize) who disagree

with me here, but if Austen was pleased by Lefroy's ability to match her in flirty games, she was less impressed
with his fashion sense. "He has but one fault," she wrote to
Cassandra, "which time will, I trust, entirely remove—it is
that his morning coat is a great deal too light. He is a very
great admirer of Tom Jones, and therefore wears the same
coloured clothes, I imagine, which he did when he was
wounded." You don't even need to know who Tom Jones is
to get the brilliance of that first line. (I've always suspected
it was a riff on Jonathan Swift—"So our Doctor has every
quality and virtue that can make a man amiable or useful; but, alas! he has a sort of slouch in his walk"—but I
also don't know whether Austen had seen Swift's letters.
A classic Janeite conundrum.)

Pause to savor this moment. Austen is knocking her
young admirer for excessive literary enthusiasm, for his
overzealous identification with a literary character; but
she's also mocking the way that young people who are
new to love will elevate minor weaknesses into terminal
character flaws: the sentence indicts young Jane, just as
much as it does young Tom. In a subsequent letter, Austen
recycles the joke; responding to a hypothetical proposal of
marriage, Austen writes: "I shall refuse him, however,
unless he promises to give away his white coat."

It's true that one comes to love these jokes because they
are, at bottom, just delightfully silly. But they are lovable,
too, because they are terribly real. I do not believe that
Austen was as horrified by Lefroy's taste in clothes as she

endeavors to sound; but I do believe that her joking criticism of his clothes had its basis in real disapproval. It's fundamentally garish behavior, in other words, to wear a blinding white topcoat just because Tom Jones did, and it's the same kind of bald affectation that nearly all of Austen's principal characters would reject, from Marianne Dashwood to Elizabeth Bennet.

It's also precisely the same kind of ridiculous and wonderful literary playacting that takes place when Janeites gather, and it remains the very thing about which Austen skeptics will mock Janeites the most: devotees of Tolstoy—or Pynchon, or Woolf—do not make a habit of treating symposia as costume parties, and this threadbare seriousness sets them apart from the lacy zealotry of the Janeites.

It is petty minds that make such distinctions, and I cannot help but feel that the Tolstoyans and Derrideans and the rest are all missing out on some of the best and cleanest fun available to an academic in the twenty-first century—not to mention the thrill, however illusory, in feeling a very real proximity to Austen's genius and her age. Such happy dislocations are impossible without the clothing and the company; if you've never rolled your eyes at a woman dressed as Miss Bates, how can you possibly expect to know how Emma felt? As Adam would later say to me: "Dressing up and going to a ball is *like* reading Jane Austen in a way that listening to an analysis of Jane Austen is *not*."

In other words, dressing as Mr. Darcy can have scholarly value, and I hope that soon departments of English across America will do the honorable thing and require one summer of Regency reenactments from any scholar seeking tenure—especially the male ones; there is, after all, still a shortage on the dance floor.

THREE

Table Talk

There are two traits in her character which are pleasing; namely, she admires Camilla, and drinks no cream in her tea.

—Jane Austen in a letter to Cassandra, January 1796

The company was seated for dinner on the second night of the camp, and as we discussed the villainous General Tinley from *Northanger Abbey*, the subject turned quite suddenly to torture.

"You know, surely," said the lady in the blue bonnet, "that Jane based the general on a real-life model?" One gentleman at the table made a face to indicate he knew where this was going and had no interest in coming along. Others nodded their heads, and the lady leaned forward, lowering her voice and glancing behind her, as though the general himself might appear at any moment.

The tale begins in farce and ends in tragedy, but the short version is that the Austens' neighbors in Hampshire included one family of straight-up villains who were deep into torture. The scion of this family was a stammering young man named John Wallop, Third Earl of Portsmouth. From childhood, when he boarded with the Austens as one of George's pupils, the earl showed signs of idiocy and occasional psychosis—one reason his family engaged trustees to oversee his estate, including the solicitor John Hanson, who was also Byron's lawyer, and who sometimes hosted Byron for hunting parties in the neighborhood.

"Of course, the English aristocracy is full of nincompoops," the lady told the table, "but Wallop was simply a fiend." As a young man, the earl rejoiced at any chance to inflict pain. He starved his servants, tormented frogs with a fork (here, one woman at the table stopped eating), and would visit slaughterhouses to whip the hogs who were about to die, telling each one in turn: "Serves you right!" Often he beat his oxen about their heads with an axe. His fascination with death was such that he would attend the funerals of strangers and, when there was not a dead stranger at hand, would have his servants stage a mock ceremony so that he could laugh at it. The earl also took to beating his servants. He pursued these pastimes with no appearance of remorse, or understanding of what remorse might mean—a bright-eyed young torture enthusiast. Or, if you join Miss Blue Bonnet's more sympathetic view, "a silly broken creature without a heart whose father probably broke him in the first place." (One woman at the table winced at this description of the madman. Another gentleman, who had not been listening, asked me to pass the bread.) When chance provided, the earl would prey on the sick or the convalescing: when one of his coachmen broke his leg in an accident, the earl waited until the doctor had set the leg, then went into the room where the man was recovering and rebroke it. His main erotic pastime involved hiring women-servants of the neighborhood to draw his blood using lancets and then carry it in a basin under their petticoats while he watched; this is also how the earl thought that insemination happened.

Even though he was almost certainly impotent, the family wanted to make sure the earl had no legitimate offspring, so, when he was thirty-one, they married him to a forty-seven-year-old woman who did her best to keep him in line while the second brother, Newton, waited to succeed to the title. During this period, Jane Austen and her family went to several dinners and balls at the Wallop family seat, and Austen's letters show no sign that she knew what the earl got up to; in one instance she notes his wife's new dress, while after another of his balls, she acknowledges that she got carried away with the wine: "I know not how else to account for the shaking of my hand to-day."

But the earl was soon to go from villain to victim. Upon the death of the earl's first wife, Hanson, the family lawyer, spirited him to London, where the lawyer then insisted on introducing his three daughters to the earl and told him to pick one. The earl chose Laura, who was deemed the prettiest, but somewhere en route to the chapel, the lawyer pulled a switcheroo, and the earl found himself shortly thereafter reciting the marriage vows not to Laura but to her elder, apparently plainer sister Mary Ann. Byron, whom Hanson engaged as a witness at the wedding, recalls that at the rushed ceremony, the earl recited his vows like a schoolboy doing Cicero—"[Portsmouth] responded as if he had got the whole by heart; and, if anything, was rather before the priest."

Byron saw the wedding as just another instance of an idiot nobleman about to enter a joyless marriage and could hardly have known that Mary Ann rivaled her new husband for sadism. She took to beating him, kept a whip under her pillow, and installed her lover in the house, a man named William Alder, who (so the servants said) would sometimes creep into bed with Mary Ann while the earl snored at her side. At one point, Alder began torturing the earl regularly and keeping him under lock and key. Eventually, the earl regained sovereignty over his own house and banished his wife, along with the three children she had produced with no help from him. In a sensational trial after Austen's death, the earl was accused and then acquitted of madness. He lived to eighty-four, and in his final years became a sort of crazed faux monarch who called himself the King of Hampshire.

A few of us had heard the story before, or part of it; the Portsmouth saga appears in Claire Tomalin's celebrated biography of Austen, but David Nokes's biography ignores the more lurid aspects, and a lot of Janeites, even if they know about the earl, have little interest—he was just a kook in the neighborhood, of little significance because the families were not close. Others, like the lady in the blue bonnet, think of the tale as a reminder that even in bucolic Hampshire lurked deception, madness, and violence so unimaginable as to verge on comic.

The table was silent after the tale was concluded. One gentleman had left his seat, and the lady who had put down her fork at the mention of tormented frogs began, tentatively, to eat once more.

"But could Jane have known?"

"Jane must certainly have known," said Miss Blue Bonnet.

"Jane could not—she writes about him in a letter, I forget which, and mentions nothing of—"

"But he was at school under Jane's father! *He boarded in their house* as a boy—"

"Exactly—back when he was just a stammering bedwetter, not the worst villain on the earth."

"So you don't think General Tilney is drawn from the wicked earl?"

"I should think the general would be much more interesting if Jane had based him on the earl. In the book he's just a coldhearted grasper."

"That's true, no one mentions him torturing the hogs."

"Or torturing the coachman!"

"Though Catherine does imagine him abusing his wife."

I entered the fray. "He does sound like a character who might have appeared in the *Juvenilia*."

Miss Blue Bonnet looked at me as though I'd just saved her family from debtors' prison. "My dear, *exactly*! I've said it myself. Where else could Jane have got the inspiration for those bloodthirsty villains?"

I demurred. "Well, Swift, for one."

The lady considered. "Yes," she said, "yes, Swift is there." She paused to sip her wine. "But you must remember that Cassandra burned a lot of Jane's letters. It is thoroughly possible"—she turned to the woman who had blanched at the frogs, and repeated—"*thoroughly* possible that Jane knew of the earl, and wrote all about him." I gave a half-bow to concede the possibility.

I was beginning to learn the secret of mealtimes in Austenworld. In some ways they offer the most gossipy and delicious interactions that world has to offer. The shared passion, the disputed biographical details, the disagreements over recipes and interpretations—these bubble during the lectures and panels but wait until a teatime pause to express themselves in full. Meals are also the most democratic part of these gatherings. At the table, one's manners are on fullest, clearest display (are you a bad listener? do you chew with your mouth open?), but digesting in company is also democratic, a reminder of equality (we are all animals together at the trough). In Austenworld, then, meals are much more about the rank and file than about the elites. Here, conversation goes to the quick, to the bold, and to those who care the most—not to those with credentials or book deals. It's anarchy, it's art, it's where the most interesting conversations happen, and where judgments are discussed, refined, and rendered without mercy.

Meals are also the moment when Janeites of all stripes—academics, civilians, and those between the two—take time to discuss manners directly, often in reference to Austen's *Juvenilia*, which contain some of my favorite scenes of etiquette, and its opposites, in all of literature. The *Juvenilia* were very much a hot topic at the summer camp. A month or so in advance, James had asked all attendees to read (or reread) the *Juvenilia*, the better to enjoy the grad students' theatricals based on these works. They're ruthless little things, hardly the sort of work we associate with the blushing maiden-aunt in Henry's biographical note. The sketches, micro-novels, playlets, and epistolary excursions included in the juvenile notebooks are all quite direct in their parodies of literary convention, but in their deepest comedy they depict the barbarities of civilized life, and how the conventions of polite conversation enable and deepen those barbarities. Most people, including a lot of semipro Janeites, have never read them. To come upon the *Juvenilia* for the first time is a revelation of disturbing hilarity. It's like discovering that, preparatory to his anatomical sketches, Leonardo da Vinci had dedicated himself to virtuosic cartoons of dismemberment: a primal comedy as prelude to a refined and civilized art. Austen wrote them all between the ages of twelve and sixteen, and for anyone who thinks of Austen as a mere stenographer of good manners, they are a life-giving tonic.

The most obvious and delectable irony of these squibs is the dissonance between the refinement of the form and the soullessness of the acts described. Observe how Austen begins *Henry & Eliza*:

> As Sir George and Lady Harcourt were superintending the labours of their haymakers, rewarding the industry of some by smiles of approbation, and punishing the idleness of others by a cudgel, they perceived, lying closely concealed beneath the thick foliage of haycock, a beautiful little girl not more than three months old.
>
> Touched with the enchanting graces of her face, and delighted with the infantine though sprightly answers she returned to their many questions, they resolved to take her home, and having no children of their own, to educate her with care and cost.

Seldom has a fairy tale about a beautiful changeling begun with such violent tyranny, so coolly described—and this deadpan, vicious sense of fun pervades the *Juvenilia*, through scenes of blackout drunkenness, gambling addiction, matricide and patricide. Nor should we forget cannibalism. Later on in *Henry & Eliza*, the heroine hurls her children out a prison window and finds herself suddenly peckish:

> But scarcely was she provided with the above-mentioned necessaries, than she began to find herself rather hungry, and had reason to think, by their biting off two of her fingers, that her children were much in the same situation.

Whenever someone tells me that Austen is the poet laureate of table manners, I refer them to this passage. Still, it does little good. You cannot argue with someone who is resolved to find Austen anodyne and safe. Austen's early fictions demonstrate experiments with voice that illuminate the technique of the later novels. In parodying the more tawdry romances of the earlier eighteenth century, Austen began to ventriloquize her own audience, absorbing convention and expectation into a voice that belongs to a sort of unthinking moral majority—the same sense of socially determined certainty that gives the first sentence of *Pride & Prejudice* its kick. These are the same entrenched norms against which Austen's heroines must contend in the "mature" novels— think Lizzy Bennet dropping the mic on Lady Catherine in Volume III of *Pride & Prejudice*. In a sad bit of irony, Austen has become so associated with Empire-waist dresses and arch table talk that for many she now *represents* a certain set of mindless norms, her novels mere wax museums of the sanitary foibles of the gentry. But Austen's mannered parrotry has always served a darker purpose, that of exploding apparently harmless social conventions that exist only to ensure the appearance of civility where none is felt, mechanisms that render everyone a hypocrite and sometimes *precipitate* the irresponsible (and unfashionable!) behavior they are meant to prevent. And yet without ritual, without community and the claustrophobia that comes with it, we can find ourselves helpless against the ancient animal instincts.

"We long for an age when people knew the rules of deportment, and followed them," James said when convening the summer camp. The men and women with whom I ate throughout the camp seemed to accept this broad notion, but a lot of them justly qualified their nostalgia. After all, this was a majority-women conference, ostensibly dedicated to conjuring a period during which few to none of them would have owned property, and many would have been married off to a dullard of a clergyman, or—like one of Austen's cousins—shipped off as a mail-order bride to an officer in the East Indies. So it makes sense that Janeites gravitate toward the *Juvenilia*, which seem to hint at this complicated, contradictory nostalgia for "order." Austen's juvenile notebooks dramatize a world of rules wherein the logic is broken. A mother notices that her children have gnawed off her fingers, and her response is merely to sigh and to make a deduction. There is a similar dismantling of apparently rational social discourse in *Love & Freindship* [*sic*], a thirty-page epistolary novella that parodies the stock melodrama of mid-eighteenth-century fantasy-romance fiction. At its heart, the passage in question is an elaborate knock-knock joke and an exercise in high nonsense that applies very well to modern-day intercourse between academics and lay readers:

> One Evening in December as my Father, my Mother and myself, were arranged in social converse round our Fireside, we were on a sudden greatly astonished, by hearing a violent knocking on the outward door of our rustic Cot.

> My father started—"What noise is that?" said he. "It sounds like a loud rapping at the door," replied my mother. "It does indeed," cried I. "I am of your opinion," said my father, "it certainly does appear to proceed from some uncommon violence exerted against our unoffending door." "Yes," exclaimed I, "I cannot help thinking it must be somebody who knocks for admittance."

> "That is another point," replied he. "We must not pretend to determine on what motive the person may knock—though that someone *does* rap at the door, I am partly convinced."

The circumstances of the larger story have little bearing on the virtuosic comedy of this tableau. ("Unoffending" and "partly" are especially satisfying.) I will merely say that the visitor is a mysterious stranger who proposes to the narrator, Laura, within four minutes of meeting her, a spoof on what the critic Marvin Mudrick calls "the lachrymose novels" of the eighteenth century. The scene is a wicked jab against certain fastidiously boring conventions of polite conversation—precisely the sort of conversations in which Austen haters suspect Janeites of being forever involved.

It is hard not to make a further deduction, like the mother who has lost her fingers: namely, that this family is utterly mad, unfit for the public, quite possibly dangerous.

Often, this fireside scene reminds me of the academic cloisters I have known, where residual high theory and subatomic specialization can preclude engagement with simple social realities—the arcane scholar or absent-minded professor more concerned with principles than with people. Scholars are parsing, deskbound creatures. Even after the partial recession of high theory and Saussurean linguistics, the public profile of the learned academic is closely associated with deconstructive instincts, "moral relativism," and every species of twenty-first-century sophistry, leaving us at once suspect and laughably shortsighted, prone to the microfixations of Mr. Collins, that cold fish who directs houseguests through his Kentish garden "with a minuteness which left beauty entirely behind." I'm not merely parroting mindless stereotypes here; any scholar of a healthily self-critical bent will see herself, on occasion, as the punch line in this fireside tableau. Laura's father is quite literally an armchair philosopher, too satisfied with his own logic games to do the decent thing and just open the door. At the summer camp, when I mentioned this scene during tea, one of our nonacademic Janeites turned to me with a look of deep seriousness. "This is the scene I picture *every time* I e-mail a hotshot professor with one of my foolish questions."

In the summer of 2008, the scholar and avowed Janeite William Deresiewicz published an essay in *The American Scholar* on "the disadvantages of an elite education," in which he complained that he didn't know how to speak with his plumber:

> There he was, a short, beefy guy with a goatee and a Red Sox cap and a thick Boston accent, and I suddenly learned that I didn't have the slightest idea what to say to someone like him. So alien was his experience to me, so unguessable his values, so mysterious his very language, that I couldn't succeed in engaging him in a few minutes of small talk before he got down to work.

"So unguessable his values, so mysterious his very language"! The thing reads like a conquistador's report from the New World. (One wonders what the plumber made of Deresiewicz.) On its publication, the piece was justly maligned for its snobbish heresies, but hardly any critics took time to praise its candor. More than a few academics have trouble socializing beyond the academy; Deresiewicz merely admitted it. It is natural to think here of Darcy 1.0, who acknowledges in the second volume of *Pride & Prejudice* that he lacks "the talent which some people possess . . . of conversing easily with those I have never seen before." In the case of Deresiewicz, the difficulty is in "conversing easily" with someone who hasn't earned multiple Ivy League degrees. At the tender age of thirty-five, an American public intellectual was forced to admit that, like Laura's father, he didn't know precisely how to open the door. From my limited experience, Austen not only encourages us to open the door—she shows us how.

It should also be noted that when a decorated Janeite neglects to open the door, whether through snobbery or through a lecture full of needlessly complicated dialectics, the hoi polloi will have words to say about it. I learned this on the first night of the summer camp, during dinner, where our conversation ranged between assessments of the chicken ("Delicious, and not at all rubbery," as one of my table companions noted with surprise); hopes and fears for the ball; and fascinated apprehension among those who would be cosplaying for the first time. But the assembly also tended to lapse into extended quotation—as I learned for the first time in North Carolina, there are few scenarios at a Janeite conclave for which attendees cannot summon a line from Austen. "Evelyn, that dress is divine, you are a paragon of fashion—" "Lud! I deserve neither such praise nor such censure," and so on.

Once we had finished dinner (those who had forgone coffee looked ready to faint), our postprandial chatter was delayed by a lecture from a distinguished professor from Duke, who told us all about "The Networked Novel and What It Did to Domestic Fiction." I thought it was grand stuff, if a bit high-flying. The nonacademics on either side of me disagreed forcibly. It had been a heady address, full of technicality and shop talk that mystified what should have been a lucid, accessible argument, and a handful of our nonacademic visitors seemed ready to fume. These objections were largely, I think, the result of the speaker's somewhat preening lexicon, which felt borrowed more from Silicon Valley than from mainline literary theory: by this account, in the eighteenth century, the domestic novel was secretly being subverted from within by something called the "networked novel"—a mode of realist fiction that unsettled easy ideas of hierarchy, of the possibility of stability in a closed community. This so-called networked novel then "disrupted" normative notions of a self-sufficient domestic world. No wonder the Janeites were ready to disrupt the speaker in question— perhaps even to expel her from the network.

At table talk perhaps more than anywhere else, the Democratic Republic of Janeites is in control—not the academic gatekeepers. This scholar had "talked down" to them, and political equilibrium would not be restored until the Janeites had prosecuted the case against her and dissipated the offensive taste left behind—a taste, apparently, that no volume of hot tea could wash away.

•

On the second night, once we had finished our discussion of the mad earl and were nearing the end of soup, conversation turned to the delicate subject of Austen fanfiction. "There's a book called *Second Impressions*," said the older lady in the blue bonnet, "and it's really quite clever." (The title is a riff on *First Impressions*, Austen's original title for *Pride & Prejudice*.)

"I have yet to read *Second Impressions*," rejoined another lady in between slurps. "But those books simply lose me when they become overtly sexual." We laughed; she didn't. "I am as happy as anybody to speculate on the domestic felicity of the Darcys, but I balk when it comes to . . ." She broke off at the most respectable point.

". . . awful sex scenes?" I offered.

"*Yes*. Awful. It just starts to feel all . . . icky."

"Like walking in on your parents," said a younger participant. The first lady considered this last remark.

"You know, I think that's true," she said. "It isn't so much that sex doesn't happen—of course it does—but the magic is somehow broken when the descriptions become so clinical, and Mr. Wickham starts to sound like something you'd watch on pay-per-view in a hotel."

"Well, now I'm curious what you've been watching when you retire to your room each night."

I found myself somewhat out of my depth in this conversation, having read only one piece of pornographic Austen revisionism, Ann Herendeen's homoerotic rendition, *Pride/Prejudice*, in which Darcy and Bingley needle each other for being gay. ("When have you ever looked at a woman but to find fault?" Bingley asks Darcy in an early chapter. "As far as marriage is concerned, my fundament is as close to a wife as you'll ever come.")

But the table was in agreement about the general boringness of Austenian smut, though we were each careful to speak sotto voce. Many of the writers who traffic in this occasionally seamy idiom will often appear at dinners like this one, and, as we learn more than once in the novels of Austen, it is important at a country assembly to pass judgment as quietly as possible. There was something coy, too, in these complaints, an implicit acknowledgment that our own respective Janeisms were no less frivolous or whimsical than the fan-fictioners', and a recognition that Janeism is a big tent that takes all kinds. The formal and informal mix together, as do high and low, Marxist analysis rubbing shoulders with culinary history and fan-fiction. Janeism is a pastiche or palimpsest, or a quilt, like the giddy genre-mix of the *Juvenilia*: deep psychology and potty humor.

The marriage of opposites is not merely an aesthetic fixture, or a plot device from the early novel—it's also a model for living and for accommodating other people; a model for withholding judgment and banishing prejudice; and a model for high-flying academics who could learn a great deal from the civilians who live just around the corner. *Pride & Prejudice* for this reason is the ideal text for bringing different stripes together. As Donald Gray wrote in 1993:

> *Pride and Prejudice*, like [Austen's] other novels, is a story about people who learn, or fail to learn, how to be, do, and recognize good in the ordinary passages of lives that would be unremarkable if Austen had not made it clear that a kind of moral salvation depends on what Elizabeth and Darcy make of themselves by learning about one another.

This is the most succinct answer to why Jane Austen's apparently modest domestic fictions carry such weight— why their appeal, at least among bourgeois readerships, is so universal and so firm. There is nothing frivolous in what we "make of [ourselves] by learning about one another"— the true frivolity is to sit around the fireside, debating epistemology instead of opening the door. As James put it to me later: "Austen is a kind of lingua franca that enables people to talk to one another."

•

At the dinners, one also began to notice the couples for whom the summer camp doubled as a romantic getaway.

Some, in the tradition of Chapman and Metcalfe, had fallen in love with each other in part through discovering a mutual love for Austen, and there are various academic power-couples across the world whose unions owe their beginning to an indiscreet moment at an Austen conference; as Kipling's narrator says in "The Janeites," Austen remains a "bit of a match-maker" even in death, and at the larger conferences I occasionally met a child conceived (the parents told me) with the aid of Austen's prose as aphrodisiac.

Most of the couples, though, are "mixed" marriages, wherein one partner (often but not always a woman) is the true believer and the other partner a willing or sporting participant. On the first evening of the summer camp, I met one such couple, a vivacious pair of sixty-somethings, the woman slim and glamorous in her bonnet and evening gown and the man stout and kindly in an officer's jacket, rarely taking his eyes off his wife, whom he regarded at all times with a smile of mingled deference and infatuation. While we sat together over a late dessert, they explained their routine. The husband had performed theater in his college days, the wife said, distinguishing himself in yellow stockings as Malvolio in Shakespeare's *Twelfth Night*. "He had never read a word of Jane," she told me, "but the first time I asked him to join me at a JASNA ball, he didn't blink—he went to have his costume fitting the very next day!"

The husband nodded at her and addressed me without

looking at me. "It is a bit like playing a role," he conceded, sounding almost bashful. "And of course we have our games—"

"He means courtship," she translated. The man grinned as if at his own foolishness and put down his cake fork.

"Sometimes we will separate before the ball, and observe one another from across the room—" he began.

His wife, unable to hold back, cut in: "—and sometimes we dance with other people!" The statement had a quality of risqué confession, and she raised her eyebrows as though we were discussing a major scandal. The husband giggled.

"She lends me out," he explained. "She won't tell you this, but I think it's because there are often so few men around, and she likes to see the women dancing."

"Liar!" she declared in triumph. "He's being very bad—the reason I have him dance with other people is so I can watch him." She squeezed his hand. "He's *very* good." Her mate shook his head.

"We've been taking lessons for some years, and I can claim only competence."

The wife persisted. "It is thrilling to watch him charm the others." They looked at each other and she coaxed him. "You can be so *charming* and I'm not sure you even know it."

"But we always end up together," the man continued, dodging the compliment. "After we've spun the room with other people, that is."

His wife leaned toward me and spoke in a stage whisper, widening her eyes suggestively: *"We always pretend that it's the first time we're meeting."*

"That actually sounds really fun," I said.

"It *is*. My friends tease me about it"—she paused and laughed—"they say that we are kinky."

"That's not what it's about," the man said quickly. "That's not why—"

She now held his hand in both of hers. "It's nothing improper, just a little game, a vacation almost . . ." She broke off and they looked at each other, and it was difficult not to think of Admiral and Mrs. Croft in *Persuasion*, one of those older couples whose mutual good humor and evident marital bliss make such an impression on Anne Elliot. Like the Crofts, this couple have no children, and like the Crofts, after many years of marriage they are still visibly in love.

After a long, private pause—for its duration there was no one in the room except for the two of them—the husband turned to me as though awaking and said: "It can be a pleasure to meet one's wife as a stranger."

The following day, while stealing a quiet moment in the shade of a tree, I spotted the wife in close conference with two other women, one on each of her arms as they traipsed across the quadrangle en route to a plenary discussion on "Mothers and Daughters in the Novels of Austen." The husband followed them at a distance of a few paces, laden with various *objets*: under his right arm, he carried a clutch of hardbound books, while his wife's reticule—a tiny period handbag—dangled from his wrist. On his left arm was a tote bag with an image of Colin Firth scowling in a frilly collar, and he busied his left hand snapping photos of the three ladies in procession. Occasionally he would stop to request that they turn around to effect a tableau. The ladies smiled and pretended to primp their hair, like Betty Boops of the Regency. Before the quartet exited my field of vision, I saw the husband bounding in pursuit of the three women, yelping a bit and waving the reticule in the air. When we bumped into each other the next day, he told me he was worried his wife had forgotten her heart pills.

"My wife's friends said I had made a spectacle of myself," he said, smiling at the figure he had cut. "Still, it would hardly have been good manners not to inquire."

FOUR

Theatricals

My uncle's barn is fitting up quite like a theatre, and all the young folks are to take their part.

> —Jane's cousin Phylly Walter, describing preparations
> for the Austen family theatricals, 1787

The first lady arrived at Pemberley that evening a quarter before seven. A declining sun warmed the room, which would become something of a furnace once the other guests had arrived. The lady, short, with gray hair like a pageboy and a tweed suit that the sunlight rendered colorless, approached us quizzically.

"Oh dear—have I missed the theatricals?"

I took as deep a breath as my waistcoat would allow. Ashley, wearing the wedding dress from her recent "semi-elopement" with her military beau, hid a smile behind her fan.

"No, but never fear—there's still time."

The lady smiled, adjusted her shoulder under a tote bag stuffed with paperbacks, and tilted her hips in a game posture. "Well, aren't you funny. I can pick out a seat then, a really *plum* seat?"

"Madam, you have your pick of the house."

It was 6:45 and curtain was at 7:00 ("curtain" here being pure metaphor), and I knew I ought to remember this woman's name because we had bantered before. The previous evening she had observed part of our rehearsal from a surreptitious perch in the back of the room; afterward she told me that watching the grad students flitting around delivering faux-tragic monologues put her in mind of the Austen family. "Isn't that just perfect," she observed. "I feel as though I've just been eavesdropping on James and Henry and all the dashing young people of Steventon—you know they used to mount plays in the rectory."

"And sometimes the barn!"

"Yes," she said with a sort of dreamy look, "and sometimes the barn. I used to act, you know; never anything so farcical as this. And have you been flirting terribly?"

I shook my head and told her that I'd been flirting rather well. She giggled. "You're all trouble," she scolded, wagging her umbrella with mock gravitas. "You'll end up just like the Bertrams, if you keep having too much fun."

The woman was correct on every score. The rehearsal she had observed was a bit of a mess, even if the players looked dazzling. Adam was sporting a darker version of my own gentleman's ensemble, with his wire glasses that lent him the air of a clergyman. Michele had rustled up a shapely turquoise Empire-waist gown, the sort of thing that could break up a marriage. And of course there was Ashley, the newlywed in ravishing white, whom we had asked to play Laura, an elaborate caricature of a wedding-crazed eighteenth-century heroine. As Ashley said during rehearsal: "I just had a surprise wedding to a soldier, so yes, I think I'm in character."

James and Inger had tasked the graduate students with staging full-costume theatricals. Our brief had been to adapt one of the tales in the *Juvenilia* to be performed on the second night of the summer camp, in the same tradition whereby young people in Austen's own time would perform popular plays, or stage adaptations of their favorite novels, for their own amusement. In the Regency, amateur theatricals offered the younger gentry a way of being literary without appearing too ambitious or pompous, while the traditional license of the theater also let them flirt openly (or "terribly"). In *Mansfield Park*, one marriage is destroyed before it ever takes place thanks to loose behavior among a group of young people putting on a semi-racy play called *Lovers' Vows*. Explaining our duties to us ahead of the summer camp, James assured us that he trusted the group to perform a respectable piece, and that any scandals arising from it would merely further the weekend's verisimilitude. He told us that flamboyant theatricals were a fixture—and a highlight—of the big annual JASNA meetings, and that if we distinguished ourselves here, perhaps we should take the show on the road.

•

The play evolved into a combination of two of Austen's teenage creations, one, *Love & Freindship*, parodying novels of sentiment and the other, *The Beautifull* [*sic*] *Cassandra*, recounting an extraordinary (and fictional) day in the life of her older sister. But the first dress rehearsal had been put off until four hours before showtime, the Blake scholar who was to deliver our prologue had yet to appear in his police uniform, and my waistcoat was making it very difficult to perform the sort of slow-breathing exercises that crisis counselors recommend in such situations.

The preparations earlier that day had been exciting and terrifying in equal measure. Michele, as our fourteen-year-old Austen, had memorized all her lines while hastening back to town from a seaside jaunt, but the rest of us were flying by the seats of our breeches and scrambling to keep all the props in order. There was a pair of Groucho Marx spectacles for the pastry chef (a minor role), a cockney's cap for the hackney-coach driver, quills and pens for the play's various letter writers, and a crucial pair of coconuts that would signal the galloping of horses.

There were also various surfaces—chairs, tables, a piano bench, a piano—on which the women were to faint, which they did frequently and with unfailing elegance. Inger's eldest daughter, Emma, all of fifteen, had agreed to play Laura's mother. She was aces, especially given that her bonnet resembled nothing so much as a collapsed flan.

The final runs were anarchy.

"Jackie, we need a beat before 'bonnet,' so the line reads, 'I had chanced to fall in love with a stately . . . bonnet belonging to the Countess of Greater Little Pymly.' Like, a big pause. An eight-months-pregnant pause."

"Where is my quill? How can I write to Isabel with no quill?"

"Ashley, we need you to go more Ophelia-on-mescaline here. That penultimate speech needs to hit the audience like a parody of every mad scene they've known."

"Ted, are you sure you can make it to the piano in time for all these cues?"

"Hey, time out, time out, rogue petticoat over here. Gentlemen, do avert your eyes."

"Please, people, when you're fainting, remember that *everyone around you is fainting.* We don't want injuries our first year."

This last bit of advice was important and could not be repeated enough—the script had turned into an orgy of fainting, and while I believe James and Inger had requested a "lively" performance, they had not specifically requested violence or injury. Indeed, their idea for the summer camp theatricals had been quite modest. They wanted us to re-create the simple, amateuristic glee of the plays that the Austen family staged at the Steventon rectory in the 1780s and beyond. "There are several miniature plays in the *Juvenilia* that might be suitable," James suggested to Adam and me when he first asked us to take charge of dramatic matters. "Really, you can practically do some of them word-for-word. That would make your job simplest."

But grad students are a masochistic lot who generally do not opt for the simplest path (witness their decision to attend grad school), and Adam and I began to think more grandiose thoughts about the possibilities of the wild and antic *Juvenilia*. We considered, and then rejected, the idea of adapting Austen's satirical *History of England* (1791; she was fifteen), not because it wasn't funny but because we didn't have enough Tudor outfits. Similarly, "The Visit" seemed at first a viable victim for adaptation— the young Jane composed it as a stage-play in the first volume of her juvenile notebooks—but its comedy is closely tied with the performance of boredom, and the play is concerned almost exclusively with table manners; the jokes, while good, would gain little from performance. That's how we came to settle on a deeply abridged version of Austen's *Love & Freindship*, a farcical novella that sends up the more absurd eighteenth-century romances, in which women are usually fainting, fleeing, or giving birth.

•

In assigning us this little dramatic task, James and Inger had given us an opportunity for a further realm of reenactment, and I credit their foresight: here we were, reenacting the very frivolities and excitements of Austen's early years—we were reliving her youth, through the words and characters that she wrote in that youth. The *Juvenilia* began, like the novels, as family performances: the family loved to read aloud to one another, and Austen's childhood pastiches entered the family's repertoire, alongside books of sermons and Johnsonian moral essays and selections from Shakespeare (much as in the Dashwood household in *Sense & Sensibility*). Later in her career, Jane would read aloud passages from her novels-in-progress. According to the critic Rachel Brownstein, as Austen read and reread her *Pride & Prejudice* draft aloud to her family and circle, the performance became "so much in demand among the friends she read it to that she pretended to fear that Martha Lloyd meant to memorize and publish it."

Janeite critics have suggested that this oral tradition within the family (a fixture among noble and genteel families of the age) is one reason Austen's dialogue in the novels feels so alive—so "spoken." As Claire Tomalin writes in her landmark Austen biography: "Her characters rarely fail to speak to one another like real people . . . There is no knowing whether the listening Austens made suggestions or criticisms; what we do know is that father, mother, and sister all had the wit to appreciate what she wrote, and to see that the promise of her early sketches was flowering into something more exceptional." The family was similarly attentive to the younger Austens' efforts at theater.

And so, in this thespian diversion, as in so much else, the division of labor at the Austen summer camp came to feel more and more like a Regency house party, with the precocious younger set mounting productions for the pleasure of their elders, whom they amuse—and shock only occasionally—with the shameless intimacy of the performance. Observing the faces of the older Janeites who spied on our rehearsals, Michele and I fancied we caught a mix of disapproval and fascinated envy. James and Inger were roundly prohibited from glimpsing the script ahead of time, and we needled them with vague hints that the production would be far saucier than it was. "We shall put the Bertrams to shame," is the most Ashley would admit to James. Once more we were stepping into the roles of a different age. There was a ghostly joy in this.

But could we match the famous confidence of the young Austen men? By all accounts—mainly letters—James and Henry had high opinions of their skills as tragedians, and their sisters and cousins would sometimes needle them for this self-seriousness. The family was joined by friends from the neighborhood, including the Fowles brothers, and they staged the tragedies in the rectory dining room. By 1784, they were doing plays in a converted barn, where early productions included *A Woman Keeps a Secret* by Susanna Centlivre, and *The Chances*, a reboot by Garrick of a quite-old English play about a reformed womanizer. (Austen may have been geographically a provincial, but culturally—especially in the realms of literature and theater—her family was reasonably hip.) The younger set seem to have enjoyed, and the older set certainly permitted, some rather edgy material—including drinking and womanizing. One of the most consistent strains of drama was the battle of the sexes. If the verbal sparring between Darcy and Elizabeth in *Pride & Prejudice* recalls Shakespearean versions of these debates (most notably Beatrice and Benedick in *Much Ado About Nothing*), it also recapitulates the gender politics over which the Austen family made so merry during the children's plays.

These theatricals, too, would have given Jane—whether in writing or in acting—her first chances to toy with the whims and expectations of an audience. The critic Penny Gay writes that Austen thrilled to "the bustle and excitement that inevitably accompanies putting on a show." The night of our performance, I noted a flush of triumph on Michele's face and wondered whether Austen's cheeks used to color like that, too. The theatricals were one more instance where Austenworld seemed to contract, to become a single living room where we were all participating in the same play—one of those peculiar magic bits of dislocation that the Janeites love so well.

•

Joe Fletcher, who would deliver our prologue in anachronistic character as a modern British policeman, appeared at the dress rehearsal with a Maglite, a fake mustache, and an unaspirated English accent on loan from Terry Jones of the Pythons. He proceeded to nail the prologue

that we had written in imitation of Shakespeare's Dogberry, full of malapropism:

SCENE: *Two writing tables bookend the room. A divan rests center stage (if possible, fainting couch). The divan should be large enough that at least two adults can faint on it comfortably at the same time. At the stage-left table sits* ISABEL; *at the stage-right table,* LAURA, *wearing wedding dress.* JANE AUSTEN, *fidgeting like a teenager, sits on the couch in the center, bored and perhaps tomboyish.* POLICEMAN *enters from rear, inspecting handbags, &c. Ted at piano, playing Schubert. Cop arrives center stage.*

PROLOGUE/POLICEMAN: [*stern*] Ladies & gentlemen, if you would please befavor me with your
silence—I am here incapacitated as a prologue,
though in the imminent dramatical dispopula-
tions, I shall be called "policeman." The playwright
has asked that I read this brief apostle: [*unfolds
paper & reads*]

"Kind audience, we pray you refrain from the
taking of snuff, the making of love, the adjusting of
bonnets, the locking-up of daughters, elopements
of any kind—and that you silence any pet birds
or . . . [*puzzled, then proud*] . . . **noble** telephones!"

The playwright also desires me to complain
that the following scenes of excitement, intrigue,
and monstrous sensibility are all deprived from

the *Juvenilia* of one Miss Jane Austen, in particular a short novel called *Love & Freindship* and an even shorter novel called *The Beautifull Cassandra*. These two tales will compete for your attention while charming your eyes, chafing your ears, and fickling your tummy bone. The playwright conforms me that the fourth wall will be broken numerous times, but that no damage will be conflicted on the building. And so, without further askew, I present: THE PLAYERS!

By the time Joe had begun his prologue, our tweedy fan in her "plum seat" had been joined by dozens of comrades, most of whom found seats of similar plumness. (The chairs were plastic; Drury Lane, this was not.) The play unfolded with very few hiccups, everyone overacting in the proper melodramatic register, and even the throwaway jokes landed as on some Richard Pryor DVD. The lines, with very few exceptions, came directly from Austen's teenage notebooks:

ISABEL: [*as though delivering a dark prophecy, or a ghost story*] Beware of the insipid vanities and idle dissipations of London, of the unmeaning luxuries of Bath and of the stinking fish of Southampton!

[*JANE holds her nose for the amusement of CASSANDRA, who giggles.*]

LAURA: But Alas! How was I to avoid those evils I should never be exposed to? What probability was there of my ever tasting the dissipations of London or the stinking fish of Southampton?

(Soon, an opportunity presents itself to Laura, in the shape of a "noble youth" named Edward and played by me.)

EDWARD: My father, you see, is a mean and mercenary wretch. Seduced by the false glare of title and fortune, this stubborn man insisted I marry Lady Dorothea. "Nay, never!" cried I. "I grant you, Lady Dorothea is lovely and engaging, and I prefer no woman to her; but know, sir, that I scorn to marry her in compliance with your wishes— [*stands up, with great piety, hand over heart*] No! **Never** shall it be said that I obliged my father."

[*The family applauds, earnestly. EDWARD bows and pivots abruptly to LAURA.*]

EDWARD: But O my Laura, whom I have loved these past four minutes beyond all strength of reason—or probability—when will you reward me with yourself?

[*Parents beam with pride.*]

LAURA: O, this very instant, my dear and amiable Edward! [*winks at* JANE]

EDWARD: Well, that's dashed convenient—your being in a wedding dress and all, I mean. [*LAURA curtsies as he kisses her hand.*]

LAURA: We were immediately united by my father . . . [*It happens quickly onstage;* CASSANDRA *throws her shredded letters like confetti.* FATHER *turns to audience with pride.*]

FATHER: For true, I had never taken orders—but [*crossing self; drawing self up*] I **had** been bred for the church!

Later, when Edward dies (I won't tell you the cause, but the coconuts came in handy), Laura delivers that wonderful madcap soliloquy, a fourteen-year-old Jane Austen's parody of Ophelia:

LAURA: Talk not to me of phaetons—Give me a violin. I'll play to him and soothe him in his melancholy hours—Beware ye gentle nymphs of Cupid's thunderbolts, avoid the piercing shafts of Jupiter—Look at that grove of firs—I see a leg of mutton—They told me Edward was not dead; but they deceived me—they took him for a cucumber.

Cassandra, meanwhile, gets her own subplot:

JANE AUSTEN: [*taking pen in hand*] O noble Cassandra, you are a phoenix. Your taste is refined, your sentiments are noble, and your virtues [*counts on fingers; gives up*] innumerable, your appearance . . . singular. [CASSANDRA *frowns*.] If the following tale afford one moment's amusement to you, every wish will be gratified of your most obedient & humble servant . . . [*grins in* CASS's *face*]—**moi**!

. . . only to wind up in the wrong story line and perish from an excess of faintings:

CASSANDRA: [*still coughing*] Take warning from my unhappy end . . . Beware of fainting-fits . . . Run mad as often as you chuse, but **do not faint** . . . [*dies*]

By the end of the proceedings, it became clear that certain males in the audience were now in love with every woman in the cast. A film of the performance would soon appear on YouTube, where it now rubs shoulders with *The Lizzie Bennet Diaries*, *The Real Housewives of Jane Austen*, and *The Jane Austen Fight Club*, among many other instances of multimedia fan-fic. Someone even filmed the Q&A session. "Is this what you thought you'd be doing when you went to graduate school?" one lady asked.

"I don't know why else you'd go to grad school," Adam said simply.

"In what form do you propose entering this on your CV?"

"'Surreptitiously,' I think is the answer," I said.

Adam jumped in. "You won't believe this, but I have a whole section on my CV devoted to period adaptations." (It's true; I'm told his Koko in the 2005 Wheaton College *Mikado* moistened every eye in the county.)

Miss Sprayberry cleared her throat: "Does the character of the policeman owe more to Shakespeare or to Monty Python?"

"Absolutely Shakespeare," I said. "He's a complete rip-off of Dogberry, though you will notice that we did not steal any of Shakespeare's lines. Very fun to write in that sort of . . . dyspeptic style."

After the Q&A, I unbuttoned my waistcoat and tasted oxygen for what felt like the first time in forty-five minutes. Several older ladies, including Tweed-and-Plum, approached me with questions, offered thanks, and informed me that I had reminded them variously of Hugh Grant and David Niven. This moment marked the climax of my fast-dwindling academic career.

•

The next morning, after a genial panel about Austen's novels on-screen, at which I appeared as a "guest film critic," the Janeites enjoyed a break of welcome refreshment called "Elevenses," a hearty spread that included scones, coffee cakes, teas, juices, fresh fruit, and several buckets' worth of clotted cream. One's impulse was to apply a straw to the clotted cream and never look back, but decorum prevailed, and we found ourselves chatting about the films, which began, of course, with the plays.

The first blockbuster stage version of *Pride & Prejudice* was the 1935 adaptation by Helen Jerome, an Australian author and critic who also had success with her dramatization of *Jane Eyre*. Jerome's *Pride & Prejudice* enjoyed sensational buzz even before its Broadway debut; during previews in Philadelphia, the play's arch dialogue caught the admiration of one audience member in particular, a man best known for never speaking a word: Harpo Marx, then forty-six years old, who saw the show two weeks before he and his brothers, with the usual assist from Margaret Dumont, premiered *A Night at the Opera*. Deeply impressed by Jerome's play, Harpo sent a telegram to his friend Irving Thalberg, head of production under Louis B. Mayer at MGM, whose wife, the actress Norma Shearer, was seeking her next project: "Just saw Pride & Prejudice. Stop. Swell Show. Stop. Would be wonderful for Norma. Stop."

According to one popular Janeite legend, Harpo's telegram set in motion a train of events that would lead to the iconic 1940 film adaptation; in fact, MGM was already plotting a *Pride & Prejudice* movie, though it's possible that Harpo's telegram inspired Thalberg to champion the project, and to cast Shearer in the main role. Still, there were various casting hiccups along the way. Thalberg died, Shearer lost the role of Lizzy—Greer Garson eventually won the part—and while Laurence Olivier now seems an inevitable choice for Darcy, the original cast in 1939 had Shearer opposite Clark Gable as the presumptive Darcy.

"How very different a Darcy he would have made," one lady said at Elevenses, referring to Gable.

"A bootlegger-patrician."

"Yes! The aristocratic gangster—his natural mode."

"If there were a *P&P* sequel, Gable would have made an excellent older Wickham."

"Or perhaps an older Willoughby."

"No! He isn't melancholy enough. Willoughby is supposed to look a bit like Chatterton, I feel, a sort of suffering poet who wandered into an inheritance."

"I could buy Clark Gable as a sensitive poet."

Several women warmed to the idea. "I'd certainly like to have seen him try."

One lady removed an iPad from a tote bag and, after a short web search, pulled up the advertisement for the 1940 film:

> *Bachelors Beware! Five Gorgeous Beauties are on a Madcap Manhunt!*

We passed around the iPad, mindful to keep it clear of the crumbs, and some of the Janeites shook their heads and muttered over the spuriousness of this advertisement. "They always feel the need to sell Austen by selling sex," one Janeite lamented. A woman at her side disagreed.

"But isn't that better than not selling Austen? The film was huge," she said simply, adding that certain Janeites of her acquaintance might never have joined the fold if the Garson/Olivier film hadn't inspired their parents to buy cheap editions of the original novels.

The lady's point was undeniable. As the film critic Kenneth Turan reminded JASNA at the society's annual meeting in 1989—several surviving cast members attended that year to celebrate the movie's fiftieth anniversary—there were five mass-market editions brought out thanks to the film, including a twenty-five-cent paperback that enjoyed twenty-one printings in the eight years following the Olivier version. American audiences may have come for the promised "Madcap Manhunt," but many of them left the theater and bought the book. However mediated one's first experience of Austen, in the end—as always—we return to the Word.

There were Janeites at the summer camp who expressed discomfort with various adaptations and reinventions that they said had taken too many liberties and thereby distorted the true Austen. Within this conservative camp, I met those who refused to watch *any* of the films, their argument being that the inevitable concessions to a mass moviegoing audience, especially an American one, were distortions that muddled the real thing; I also met those who frowned on explicitly cheeky efforts, such as Amy Heckerling's brilliant retelling of *Emma* in the film *Clueless*, or even YouTube pastiches such as *The Lizzie Bennet Diaries*. The seemingly limitless options for fan-fiction, unofficial sequels, and so forth are a real source of anxiety to some people who distrust the apparent infinitude of possible Janes. They worry that too many people now discover Austen through the movies, and that such people end by confusing the movies for the books. Or, as one Janeite put it to me: "I worry that people will decide to rewatch *Bridget Jones's Diary* rather than reading *Pride & Prejudice*."

Still, I found it hard to share these concerns in any lasting way; far more persuasive were those hard-core Janeites who nonetheless exulted in the open-source way that Austen has of giving us limitless possibilities for re-imagining the author. As one woman remarked over the clotted cream, plenty of people in the Victorian age read Shakespeare first through the synoptic work of Charles Lamb, while more than a few medievalists say that their first contact with the material that became their life's work was a childhood viewing of *Monty Python and the Holy Grail*. "It's the same as *Clueless*," another woman interjected. "I showed the Heckerling movie to my daughter, and she promptly read *Emma* in a single day." For foreign viewers (added the woman who spoke of Charles Lamb), film versions such as *Kandukondain Kandukondain* (*I Have Found It*), a Tamil adaptation of *Sense & Sensibility*, or the Bollywood-inflected *Bride & Prejudice*, might offer the first glimpse of a world they will then rediscover when they open the books in translation.

This more optimistic view struck me as wise, and I was encouraged by the idea that one can enjoy apocryphal Austens without losing track of the original; that, in fact, engaging with others' conceptions of Austen brings you closer to the real thing. The profusion of possible Janes, the infinitude of Austens (one pictures them amassed like a Roman legion) gives options to the modern reader: *Here's how other people have found access to Austen, and discovered her on their own terms.* It is right and good, goes this account, to make your own version and play with various ideas of Jane. The author is more powerful than her mediators, and will always overcome them. This striving toward the original is the work of textual editors from Chapman to Claudia Johnson, but it's also the province of fans. It is why we study Austen's fiction together, why we rewrite and subvert it, and why we enact it onstage wearing anachronistic wedding dresses and fake mustaches. Through the imagined possibilities of what she might have been, we involve ourselves, however whimsically, in discovering who she really was.

The Janeites who were huddled around the tea table had their disagreements, but the tone remained attentive and cordial: a band of rational siblings, negotiating yet another small codicil in a shared literary inheritance, all over crumbs and cream.

If the summer camp allowed us to dramatize Austen's *Juvenilia*, her juvenile notebooks themselves dramatize the hyperbole of sentimental literature that Austen clearly read by the basketful, and in which she found ample material for tuning her gifts of literary parody and moral satire. While the *Juvenilia* are off-color, coarse, and concerned with drunkenness and occasional cannibalism, they are best and most simply described as theatrical: they are overblown; characters do not experience scenes so much as perform them; and most important, the epistolary novellas are funniest as dialogue, which I suspected but didn't discover until Adam and I began the adaptation. Looking at the theatrics of the *Juvenilia*, even the nondramatic works, you begin to appreciate (and soon to adore) how Austen is examining, enjoying, and testing the limits of the most popular sensibilities and forms of her day: that is, the heroic picaresque or sentimental romance, delivered in histories, plays, playlets, novels, letters.

It's here that you suddenly start to realize how Jane Austen developed the mature craft that has bewitched all these people. To understand Austen—and thereby understand Janeism—you must understand the *Juvenilia*. In every one of these, Austen's youthful energies overwhelm the form and exhaust the performance of emotion—yet they remain controlled performances, every bit as controlled as the later, more emotionally continent novels. The Janeite who has been awakened to the playhouse inflections in those novels can return to the *Juvenilia* and observe how

Austen joyously dismantles the histrionic conventions of sentimental literature, sending up her favorite books by rendering their subtext in surreal dialogue: *Run mad as often as you chuse, but do not faint!*

Once the video of our summer camp performance appeared on YouTube, I began to get odd requests via e-mail, phone, and even letter. One woman called to ask whether I could tutor her children in "the ways of Jane Austen." Another wrote me a long letter to ask for help in preparing a coffee-table book about Jane Austen and theater. Two parents in Canada asked whether the grad-school players would be willing to stage a one-act that their daughter had written. And Syrie James, author of historical fiction and several Janeite pastiches, asked whether I would come play Henry Crawford—a charming and quite wicked character in *Mansfield Park*—for a play she was preparing with Diana Birchall at the following year's general meeting of JASNA, to be called *'A Dangerous Intimacy': Behind the Scenes at Mansfield Park*. This last request was in many ways typical of my time in Austenworld: as a young man who cleans up nice and can recite Austen when properly motivated, I met certain minimal requirements and was thereby elevated to a sort of absurd exoticism. I was again enjoying the affirmative action afforded to the men of Austenworld, in being asked to play a handsome but fundamentally dangerous gentleman—flattering and false.

"Henry Crawford is a smooth operator," I wrote to

Syrie. "I fear you may be giving me more credit than I deserve."

"Yes, perhaps," Syrie responded. "Or perhaps less."

When a Janeite asks you for a favor in service to the Cause, there is only one proper answer, and at the AGM in Montréal the following year, you would have seen me onstage as Henry Crawford, acting scenes from *Mansfield Park* and flirting outrageously with the Maria Bertram character, played by Syrie herself. Syrie's husband (who, to confuse matters further, was playing her father) watched from the wings of the banquet hall as Syrie and I stroked each other's faces and pantomimed a very un-Austenian makeout scene. In a final apocryphal stroke, Syrie arranged for a ruddy-faced English gentleman to play the Prince Regent, who swept onstage at the end of the play to make a couple of racy jokes and to steal Maria from me, to the delight of the several hundred Janeites in the room. The prince was the one character who could upstage Henry Crawford—and the permanently smiling man who played him was Patrick Stokes, a direct descendant of Jane's younger brother Charles. The theatricals at the North Carolina camp had taken us to the heart of the Austen household of Jane's youth; now, in Montréal, I was face-to-face with that family, the living legacy of her blood. I wished that Adam or Ashley or Michele could be there to enjoy the brief moment with me where we had no need of Claudia Johnson's ghost—Austen's DNA was quite literally with us.

FIVE

The Ball

Like the Bennets, the Austens took a relaxed view of what it meant to be out. This was the country; the Austen daughters had been joining in country dances at home from their earliest years, and knew all the neighbours' sons and daughters; children took part in dancing, brothers danced with sisters, girls with one another. —Claire Tomalin

She enjoyed dancing, and excelled at it.

—Henry Austen, 1818

I should say—indeed, I would disgrace myself as a narrator if I pretended otherwise—that Austenworld was not always a comfortable place. This might seem odd, given how warmly I was received into that world, how quickly my shortcomings were forgiven or ignored, how generously everyone taught me their recipes and dances, and shared with me the versions of Austen that seem, to them, most real. These are all deep intimacies, and I remain unworthy of many of them. Austenworld was kind to my academic career while giving me ample material for magazine freelancing, but I knew that at some point there would be a reckoning—I have been told that there is no such thing as a half-Janeite, just as there's no such thing as a half-scholar. Yet in the end, I turned out to be both.

"You must be a great comfort to your mother, sir," I was told on various occasions—a corruption of Mrs. Allen's line to Henry Tilney in *Northanger Abbey*. This was true. But I could never escape the feeling of also being a fraud. The Janeites' love of the author, their expert and honestly gained knowledge of her age and its manners, their delights in dances that bored me after an hour or so—these all came to feel like an accusation, an indictment, of my own dilettantism. Whereas the others at Camp Austen had discovered Austen themselves, for me she was merely an inherited or even genetic eccentricity; a set of allusions; an affectation; a second language that I spoke carelessly and would likely never master. For I am hardly an *intrepid* Janeite, as Chapman was in Macedonia; still less was I a *worshipful* Janeite, like Forster with his Bloomsbury panegyrics to the novelist; nor a *snooty* Janeite, like Henry James—I do not wish to protect her from the masses, nor the masses from her. Unlike Harding, I am fairly untroubled by misreadings or by the soft, acritical self-congratulation of the Janeite in company. In other words, I have no loyalty. I am, indeed, a half-Janeite by blood, one who hasn't attended an Austen function in more than eighteen months at the time of this writing, a Janeite who knows the novels and the major criticism quite well but who unforgivably does not particularly enjoy *Emma*, widely regarded among true connoisseurs as the height of Austen's technical achievement. (Which it is—but I'd still rather read *Persuasion*.) In dark moments, during my time in Austenworld, I would reflect that it was largely accidents of birth, and dislocation, that made it possible for me to perform Janeism like a parlor trick. A different choice of graduate school—or a mother with healthier knees—would have sunk my chances altogether.

When friends have asked why I no longer frequent this world, I have avoided an explanation that I assume they cannot understand: that I became increasingly uncomfortable with the affirmative action that I continued to receive in Austenworld, whereby a straight, quasi-eligible male represents a desirable minority. From a literary standpoint, this weird return to the normative ideal of the patrician hero is understandable nostalgia, but from a political standpoint, it's utterly reactionary. The age when such men could be heroes has passed, and even if it hasn't, such a role is not for me.

Reading Austen helps keep you aware of your hypocrisies and vanities. Increasingly, I felt like a hypocrite when I put on the clothes, pretending to the honest enthusiasms of someone else. There are many paths to the one true Jane—many Janeisms rather than a single prescriptive orthodoxy—and mine is not the world of reenactment; it is the quiet moment reading *Persuasion*. Still, even if you're no more than an accidental Janeite—an imperfect reader or a bad dancer who is sometimes so selfish that he skips the *whole ball* because he knows if he hears the Dashwood family name one more time he'll have a nervous collapse— even for such lost souls, there is a place in the inheritance, a good set of clothes, a seat at the table, a role in the action, and (most important) a partner at the ball, even if she's just a three-foot-tall version of Fanny Price in miniature.

I stand before you a failed Janeite.

Which is to say, a Janeite.

Arraying my costume ahead of the ball, I looked at the garments and winced slightly—what an odd figure I was about to cut—and then I thought of Chapman, whose example chastened me: if he could write for the *TLS* with bullets whizzing past his ears, why was I staring at this costume as though it were a Turk who wished me ill? I removed all items of twenty-first-century clothing and descended into the tights. The occasional frantic yelp would emanate from the ladies' room next door. Man- fully, I closed the barn door of my breeches and exited the water closet. "Ashley? Is everything—okay?"

Ashley's head slowly appeared around the door she was clutching like a shield.

"Ted! Wardrobe malfunction."

There ensued a pause, as Ashley evaluated my delicacy, and I evaluated my ability to help.

"Perhaps you could—"

". . . find Michele?"

"That would be lovely."

Michele was duly summoned and gave me a gentle look as she entered the ladies' room, a sort of consolatory smile. "Don't take it personally," is what the look said, and I didn't. A man who can barely clothe himself will hardly bridle at the suggestion that he isn't an expert in women's apparel. Before long, several female colleagues had entered the bathroom and converged on Ashley, later assuring me the process was similar to the scene in *Cinderella* where the birds flock to the heroine and prepare her for the ball.

By comparison, Adam and I faced more modest difficulties. He helped me with my "foolproof" cravat, and we considered ourselves in the mirror.

"Bingley, good man."

"Darcy! Second soul to my own."

"Shall we away?"

"Yes." Adam smiled. "High time we meet our new neighbors. To the ball?"

To the ball.

•

The Meryton Assembly began at 7:00 p.m. the final evening of the camp. The heat of late June abated very little, and my principal fear was that, during the ninety-second walk between Pemberley and Gerrard Hall, I would drench my four layers (even the wool topcoat!) with the telltale sweat of a nervous neophyte. An inventory seemed appropriate. Top hat? *Check*. Cocked eyebrow and snooty expression? *Check*. Reporter's notebook that will double as my dance card? *Check*. Ashley, a vision of eighteenth-century marriageability, materialized in her new gown and was now as convincing a Caroline Bingley as any TV or film adaptation has given us. She gave her "brother" (Adam) a kiss on the cheek and curtseyed to Darcy (me), adding a very patrician wink. Well done, Miss Bingley. Well done indeed.

The brain trust had instructed us to enter fifteen minutes late and fifteen miles aloof, in direct imitation of the Mertyon Assembly scene in Joe Wright's 2005 *Pride & Prejudice*. As we met en route to the dance hall, Caroline with Adam on her arm, I removed my top hat and bowed so low that the breeches popped a button, and our exotic little party proceeded ball-ward. Outside Gerrard, we met one of my undergraduate students, Nathan, a talented young writer with an intense fondness for David Foster Wallace. Nathan was handing out programs and serving as usher in his capacity as an intern for the Theater Department, and his glee in my raiment was unbounded. Nathan would later circulate several photos of this moment to a coterie of my journalism students. Like all tourism, time travel has its inevitable minor embarrassments.

As our music cue approached, it was time to get in character. Our brains addled from heat, little sleep, and too many panels, we reverted to utter parodies. Adam's wife, Blanche, looked on as Ashley and I offered pitying pronouncements about "poor Charles."

"Oh, Mr. Darcy, what tiresome company this evening will afford us." (Her Caroline Bingley was very good.)

"Indeed—why Charles insists on laying hands on the local peasantry has always baffled me."

Adam was a saintly good sport about the whole thing.

"I say, Darcy, I intend to dance with every young lady in the neighborhood tonight," he simpered. "Every last one of them. How I *do* love a ball."

"Why confine yourself to the neighborhood, Bingley? Surely there is some stable-girl in a nearby shire whom you have yet to call a goddess."

"Oh, Darcy, you . . . you *so-and-so*."

Caroline and I then whispered behind her fan about its being past Charles's bedtime. You'll pardon this descent into caricature, I hope. We used real lines as well, of course, though it was all dangerously casual, and I did not feel entirely comfortable delivering Darcy's snide (and racist) proclamation "Every savage can dance," which passed my lips only once that evening. Nor did I dare to employ Aldous Huxley's variation on this bit of dialogue in his 1940 screenplay of *P&P*: "Any *hottentot* can dance," a line that heightens the ugly colonialist hauteur by virtue of specificity. The Janeites assembled outside the dance hall seemed pleased if unsurprised by our approach and even flattered us with an ovation, though at the door I was justly chastised by two women for smiling too much. "Mr. Darcy has no business looking so happy," one of them told me.

A Regency cotillion is well worth observing if you ever get the chance. The floor should be rectangular or square, with plenty of room for at least two dozen couples to stand in two rows, facing each other over a distance of five or so paces. The action is graceful, even when performed by amateurs: as with line dancing, it's a collective effort, and best viewed from a balcony. Seen from above, partners separate and recombine in new configurations (now a spinning quartet, jigging in a circle; now an octet, followed by a sudden return to your original partner), as the dancers describe curlicues, and the whole affair becomes a series of larger themes and smaller grace notes—a kaleidoscope wherein humans are the crystals. Over the course of a Janeite ball, the company invariably becomes familiar with each of the antiquated group dances, helped in no small measure by the liberating effects of wine-punch, and by the presence of Jack Maus at the head of the room, calling out the steps and exhorting the revelers "not to be shy."

•

As the last note of the third number redounded and died, our little trio entered the great hall. I removed my hat and Ashley lowered her fan, both of us appraising the company with as much disdain as we could muster in the giddy spirit of the moment. Muttering began among the Meryton gentry. Jack Maus, *maître de la danse*, handed me a microphone.

"It is, I must say, a . . . *singular* pleasure to be among you this evening. Your facility at the cotillion is rather good. For the provinces."

Adam took the mic and began calling every person and inanimate object "charming," including as many superlatives and uses of "I say" as the Queen's English allowed. Maus then requested that Caroline Bingley and Mr. Darcy lead the following dance. We assented. As Maus prepared the string quintet, Inger's youngest daughter, Clara, tiny and dressed in lovely Regency white with a pink sash, asked whether she might dance with Mr. Darcy. Her face was a beautiful crimson. I took a knee to explain that my second dance was spoken for, but would she do me the honor of saving the third? She nodded her bonny blonde head in agreement, and would of course keep me to my word. Ashley labored to preserve her deportment of condescension even as we "led" the next two dances and linked arms happily with various delightful people on whom Darcy and Miss Bingley, drunk on their own excellence in the first volume of *Pride & Prejudice*, expend so much disdain.

There is a pleasant geometry to these Regency cotillions: a refreshing alternation between the basic circle and the basic oblong or square. So, for instance, if Caroline Bingley and I are the lead couple at the head of the dance line, we will perform various curlicues: spinning one another, lacing ourselves between and then around the "B" couple, just below us, and of course doing the "back-to-back," which is the rural English equivalent of the rural American "do-si-do." We then proceed, in linear fashion, down the line of two dozen–ish couples, until the "head" couple finds itself at the bottom. Not unlike the end of *Mansfield Park*, really.

Our twenty-first-century difficulty with the steps put us very much at odds with the Austens, their circle, and their contemporaries around England, for whom these dances, though they depend on a rich geometry, were essentially second nature—one of Austen's biographers suggests that the family could have done all the jumping, setting, circling, and promenading with their eyes closed.

Despite Ashley's enthusiastic fainting at the instruction earlier that day, she had been paying close attention, and had achieved a graceful command of her moves that allowed me to "follow" without disgracing myself. There are moments at a cotillion when even the fleetest of foot will find him- or herself mimicking Wile E. Coyote, racing in blushingly belated manner through old steps in a doomed effort to catch up with the micro-orchestra. In one moment of particular shame, Ashley watched with patience as I twirled myself in a half-assed way to make up for not having twirled *her*.

"I think we're doing all right, Darcy," she said with a smile. "See how the natives positively teem with admiration."

I smiled in response and said nothing, lest I fall further behind. I comforted myself with this thought: whatever I lacked in precision and training, I might recoup via twirls of the foot, the occasional soft-shoe, and easy manners.

Clara proved an equally forbearing partner. Her blushes dissipated as the hornpipe began; before long, she was issuing gentle correctives in my direction:

"No, this way"; "Now you must take my hand"; or, more often, "This way, Mr. Darcy!"

Clara is in some respects an anomaly among American primary-schoolers, the early beneficiary, much like Georgiana Darcy, of a family devoted in equal measure to fine books and fine hospitality. But her language here is so curious that it bears brief comment. We have spoken before about dress and company, and how these two can adjust character and behavior. The anachronistic directive "Now you must take my hand" is a lovely example; however bookish and well-mannered, Clara was speaking through inherited, unrehearsed formal patterns of speech, likely culled from early exposure to Austen adaptations on-screen, recalled by the circumstances of the ball, and energized by the period outfit.

We enjoyed two such dances together, my tiny tutor and I, and photographs of the proceedings will comfort me in my golden years. Several hours and many minuets later, I would see the young lady fast asleep across the chest of her smiling father. Dozy adults were weary from booze; this little sylph was merely exhausted from having kept me in line for so long.

Having acquitted myself through several rounds of dance without face-planting, I saw no objection to repairing to the viewing gallery for idle gossip and decorous flirtation. Whist had been on the evening's docket, but dancing monopolized the collective attention, along with bowl after bowl of Shrub, a vinous punch concocted in the classic style by Gary Crunkleton, a local bar owner and "mixology historian." I abstained, but the ladies in my company assured me the concoction was divine. It became curiously clear, in this moment, how very easy it might be to find oneself smitten on such a night, two-hundred-some years ago.

A few hours later, in the kitchen of an unfamiliar house, I quietly separated my 1813 clothes from my 2013 clothes and slipped the latter onto my weary limbs. My suit pants felt as billowy as a sundress, and this sensation lingered as I whispered parting words and then tiptoed home to prepare for the closing ceremonies, which would begin shortly after the imminent sunrise. (The words would resonate, and the house would not long remain unfamiliar.) Seeing my "costumes" side by side, a happy thought entered my still-twirling head. We do not dress to escape ourselves; we dress to clarify ourselves through the crystal patterns of a half-recovered world where seeking goodness in others creates goodness in turn—where finally, beneath the starch and the silly outfits, we find some long-forgotten piece of our true, our best selves.

The Carolina dancing prepared me insufficiently for my first JASNA meeting in Minneapolis, where I went following my partial conversion to Janeism at the summer camp. Once more, I was an unworthy surrogate for my mother—my tasks in Minneapolis included delivering one of my mother's papers while she lay on a couch in upstate New York with her legs elevated—but I was also on assignment, still writing about, and trying to understand, the Janeites, this intoxicating secret society that was beginning to feel like an unexpected birthright.

My dancing in Minneapolis showed certain improvements. Though still clumsy and inattentive to choreography, I was at least not a total amateur the second time around. Nevertheless, the size alone of the annual JASNA meeting meant the ball would be far more populous, collisions would be more frequent, and no one was safe from a camera. As the ball was set to begin, the writer Deborah

Yaffe dragged over a friend, the two of them insisting that "Jane Bennet" (a gorgeous historical novelist with bouncy blonde ringlets) had been eyeing me.

"Go over there!" Yaffe told me. "Tell her she's the very image of Jane Bennet. That's your line."

I thanked Deborah and turned to locate the woman in question, who had just materialized on my right arm.

"They're taking photographs of us," she whispered into my ear as she steered me toward a phalanx of camera-phones. "I hope you don't mind." Her poise before the cameras, and the commanding way in which she had taken my arm, felt absurd, like a moment of stage management on a red carpet outside the Oscars. There were camera flashes all around us, and I didn't even get to use Deborah's line before the lady had reserved two dances with me. Things were looking up.

At dinner, while scribbling observations in my steno pad, I noticed Inger and Emma Brodey seated two tables away in the banquet room. After the chicken course, Inger spotted me, smiled, rose, and approached.

"Ted, at the risk of meddling, I should like to say that the two ladies on either side of me would both be tickled if you reserved the first four dances for them."

Craning, I spotted them: Prashansa, a young Indian scholar in a crimson sari, and Maria, a young Colora-doan with doe eyes and lashes the length of Samuel Richardson's *Clarissa*. Maria wore a beautiful white gown with a red sash.

"Of course, Inger. Depend upon me. Shall I pretend we never had this conversation?"

Inger almost giggled. "Yes, I think we'd better."

Staff began clearing tables to make room for dancing, and I approached the women in question.

"Excuse me—I wondered whether you ladies would do me the honor of reserving the first portion of your dance cards for me."

They smiled—Maria actually curtseyed—and agreed, with a sly glance at Inger.

We were novices, and there were one or two moments when our costumes came between us (the breech-clasps below my knees kept coming undone, while Prashansa's sari did its best to trip her graceful feet), but no one trod on anyone else's toes, and we acquitted ourselves well. Conversation during the "Duke of Kent's Waltz" was quite literally by the book.

"And now it is your turn to talk," Prashansa told me, as we spun down the dance line. I lost only a moment in finding my bearings—*Pride & Prejudice*, Volume I. She's Elizabeth. You're Darcy. Get on it.

"Perhaps something about the number of couples?"

"Yes!" Prashansa cried. "Or the size of the room!"

Maria's dress was far better behaved, an arrangement that left her free to bat her eyes at a rate that would turn any warm-blooded man epileptic.

"You're very good, you know," I told her.

"Don't tell anyone I didn't attend the instructional

sessions," she stage-whispered. We interlaced with other couples, parted, reunited at the center of the dance line.

"It's so crowded!"

"I would have twirled you, but there wasn't sufficient real estate."

"Oh, we can twirl next time; just don't let Glasses over there step on your toes."

Deborah Yaffe and her partner appeared next to us, in one of the kaleidoscopic reconfigurings that form the ritual intricacy of the Regency assembly-dance.

"I see you're doing well for yourself," Deborah said.

"You as well," I said.

"But what happened to Miss Bennet?"

"Miss Bennet, sad to say, is married." (This was true.) "But I really must thank you for your matchmaking efforts."

Deborah pulled me aside for a moment. "Well, at least we know," she said in a tone of delectable conspiracy.

As a break in the proceedings, the staff refreshed us with meats, cheeses, and white soup, the latter a favorite with Charles Bingley. ("As soon as Nicholls has made white soup enough I shall send round my cards," he promises Lydia before the Netherfield ball.) Making my way toward a table, I came upon a group of women discussing their conquests at previous years' balls. "I've tried to explain to my cousin," said one lady. "Nobody comes here for the sex. But we're warm-blooded people—"

"I like to watch a man struggle with a corset."

"It's like you get the best of then and now! You can dress like Emma but still go to bed with Frank Churchill."

"Assuming his fiancée isn't around."

The women agreed that a JASNA ball was a bit like visiting a resort in Austen's day, when, as a tourist in Bath or Southampton, a man or woman of means could behave much more freely than at home, especially given that most people would be strangers.

"Do you think Austen would have considered Minneapolis a resort city?"

"I don't know, but we're here, and we're thoroughly disguised."

"Imagine just putting your hand down Willoughby's pants. What a power move that would be."

"I think one's allowed a bit of fun after being so studious all day."

"I should think Jane would be happy to see modern ladies getting to enjoy themselves, though I'm not sure she'd be impressed with the selection of men . . ."

I sat myself with Maria and Prashansa and several older ladies. The lady to my right, in a green bonnet, offered us a gracious smile as we installed ourselves.

"Oh, I know you—I attended your mother's talk," said Miss Green Bonnet. "She seems to have the proper idea about Austen and sex."

"Your mother had many thoughts on this score," Prashansa said with a smile.

"My mother," I explained to Maria, "disagrees with Ruth Perry, who argues that film adaptations have blinded us to Mr. Collins's status as an eligible bachelor." Maria laughed.

"Yes, *that* is going too far. But the films always make us read the books differently, don't they?" The table issued nods and slurps. "For instance: Do you like the Olivier/Garson version?" Maria was referring to the 1940 version, directed by Robert Z. Leonard with a script by Aldous Huxley and Jane Murfin. (The one with the "hottentot" line.)

"I do, very much," I said with a generous wave of my soup glass. "Despite its famous liberties!"

Maria nodded. "Which include a thorough rewrite of Lady Catherine."

"A public rehabilitation in the third act?"

"Indeed. And of course that's all a wartime thing—the American *P&P* leaves us with warm feelings toward this crusty exponent of the traditional gentry virtues."

"Right. Because we'd never send troops to help Mrs. Norris," someone added.

The evening's wines were beginning to take effect; this remark was met with titters around the table. I told the ladies about the man whom I had met in the elevators that morning. There were two conferences happening concurrently at the Minneapolis Hilton: JASNA, and a separate, much smaller weekend seminar called "Financial Planning for Lutherans." In general, it was not difficult to tell which hotel guests were attending which of the two conferences. The gentleman in question (who struck me as the very model of a fiscally prudent Lutheran) had cast a smiling eye over the dresses and petticoats in the lobby of the hotel before joining me in the elevator to observe that "everyone seems to be dressed very nice."

I laughed, uncertain as to what he meant, whether he was joking. "What do you think of the bonnets?"

"Well, I guess I didn't realize they were back in fashion!"

He wasn't joking.

"You realize it's the big annual meeting of the Jane Austen Society?"

His smile widened but he remained blithe, unfazed. "Oh! How funny. I had no idea. I thought perhaps there was a wedding or baptism."

When I returned to North Carolina, I was telling colleagues in the English Department all about my first JASNA meeting, making sure to include the vignette of this God-fearing man and his blissful lack of astonishment at the finery of the Janeites. "Perhaps that's how we'll know the Janeites have won," one professor offered. "When you can walk down a city street dressed like Lizzy Bennet and nobody even thinks to give you a second look."

My second and final JASNA was the one in Montréal the following year, where I had agreed to play Henry Crawford and where, fitted with bionic knees, my mother joined me at last—no longer was I a surrogate, but merely (and much more happily) a companion. After her conspicuous absence at the summer camp and at the JASNA meeting in Minneapolis, it seemed only fitting that we should attend at least one big Austen shindig together. I was eager to observe my mom being fêted by past students and old collaborators, to count her admirers, and to bask in her reflected glory. I was also beginning to suffer from a case of Janeite fatigue, the sense that I had become little more than a fancy eavesdropper, and, far from blaming me for this lack of proper spirit, my mother seemed to understand. At the Montréal conference, we were a little Janeite universe of two, mixing freely and volubly with those Janeites who were not linked to us by blood, but largely keeping to ourselves, in what was a temporary breach of the local etiquette. After our dinner and the annual "toast to Jane" (during which the gathering feels much like a séance), I asked Mom whether she felt up to dancing. She gave me a wonderful frank look.

"If you're asking whether I can physically stand it," she responded, "then the answer is yes."

"But?" I suspected we were both harboring the same shameful secret.

She leaned over to whisper in my ear so that our tablemates wouldn't hear us.

"I am so exhausted, and I do not need to dance 'Mr. Beveridge's Maggot' right now."

Deeply relieved, I told her that I felt the same. I looked around the room, spotted Julia Matson (founder of Bingley's Teas, proprietrix of that "loose woman" poster), and knew that she would castigate me if I fled dancing-duties. Julia and I had walked through the old city earlier that day, and I had basically sworn up and down that I would participate, with enthusiasm, in the ball. Prashansa and Maria had not repeated their appearance from the previous year, but there were other people in the room to whom I had suggested, if not promised, that I would take a spin with them. But I was tired, and in love to distraction with someone who wasn't on the continent, and I had precisely zero patience for flirtation of any sort. I was being a horrible Janeite, doubly so because I represented an endangered species, and by absenting myself would further exacerbate the shortage of men. These considerations did little to cool my conscience, but it was my mother's judgment that most concerned me, and since she had approved my plan to flee, I was resolved.

We retreated to the hotel room that we were sharing. Before long, my phone started to jangle with text messages informing me that I had been derelict in duty. Some of these were quite direct: "My dear Mr. Crawford—I had expected that you would grace us for at least two dances, and your absence is unaccountable." I asked my mother's blessing to use her fatigue as an excuse, and she consented. In a text to one correspondent, I remarked that Austen's novels tend to illustrate the virtues of filial duty. The lady was unmoved: "There are other women with claims on your time."

Meanwhile, my mother asked that I unzip her dress. I obliged, and she laughed. "I guess this isn't how you figured the night would play out," she said over her shoulder. I acknowledged the joke, and we sort of chuckled and then watched an episode of *Foyle's War* before falling asleep, in separate beds, my phone still buzzing.

•

A lady once described to me her first impressions on visiting Austenworld: "Finally, a place where one can be oneself." For all the contradictions implied therein, the statement is true. For all the affectation, the Regency dialogue and borrowed postures, there is a holy frankness to the proceedings, a general sense of, well, let's give this a go—let's go mad a bit and argue over who stole the turkeys in *Emma*. Let's stroll through the quadrangle with parasols and lose ourselves in a better world that never existed. Austen-mania is a collective folly, a religion in the sort of latitudinarian-Anglican sense that stresses communion over orthodoxy (though it is possible to be excommunicated). It is a shared fiction that we tacitly agree to treat as real, and by coming together we make it real. At some point, for me, participating in this fiction became impossible, coming to represent a destined thing, rather than one that I felt in my bones I truly belonged to. This was my mother's world, and I was living out the plot that she had set in motion twenty years ago. Yet, even as a failed Janeite and a lapsed scholar, I am grateful that my sojourn on her behalf rekindled my mother's love for Austenworld. Indeed, her love of that world has perhaps never been this deep. Austenworld is a space of contemplation, listening, kindness, and wonder—a paradise in which I was unworthy to remain but the memory of which I will cherish always.

I visited James last summer in North Carolina. He took me out for lunch and told me all about the previous month's camp, where my mother had made an appearance as speaker, and where Michele—this time dressed and in character as the wicked Mary Crawford from *Mansfield Park*—had proceeded to argue with my mother about Charlotte Lucas. James told me how his summer project was looking after his infant granddaughter five days a week—they would go on walks and build things, and as he told me about these simple joys I couldn't help but think that *this* was what Mr. Bennet could have been with less pride, less laziness, a greater capacity to *act* on his love. And perhaps what is more, that here was a true Janeite—the man who values people more than books, who is not too shy or lazy or proud to live fully in a fallen world; who does not suffer from manners envy and does not romanticize the sense of prelapsarian self-recovery that pervades Austenworld;

who would rather bound across campus with a tiny girl than sit, and teach, and administer from some academic fastness.

In thinking about Austen, I cannot separate the notion of community from the notion of voice—that bewitching, crystalline narrator's voice, the voice that shares so much with Elizabeth Bennet's idea of a "rational creature." Naturally, the narrator figure, the Jane, is the real allure of the novels. I think again of the first sentence of *Pride & Prejudice*—a sentence that, like so much of Austen's sly, slippery management of her material, *appears* to depend on a mutually agreed-upon set of assumptions among Right-Thinking People: "It is a truth universally acknowledged . . ." But the joke of each novel is that these truths *aren't* universal. Characters who fail to modulate a rigidness in their way of thinking, who leave their mannered prejudices uninterrogated, are the ones in need of correction. Assumptions—about how to act, even how to think and feel—are just that: assumptions. Rather than being "universally acknowledged," truths must be mutually negotiated, among those whose moral intelligence will admit correction, and on the premise that kindness and curiosity and care will lead to understanding.

In a few years, the Jane Austen Summer Program will run out of novels. They will nonetheless persevere. There will be as much to rediscover in *Pride & Prejudice* in 2020 as there was in 2013. If my math is correct, young Clara

Brodey will then be in high school, old enough to run the theatricals herself. My fondest and most selfish hope is that she will remember one summer when she was shorter than the grass, and Mr. Darcy did his best to keep up with her at the ball.

ACKNOWLEDGMENTS

The occasional glibness of this volume makes me hesitant to implicate others. Nonetheless, I am deeply indebted to my doctoral committee—Eric Downing, Megan Matchinske, Thomas Reinert, Jessica Wolfe, and James Thompson—for supporting my nonacademic pursuits during a year's leave and then for not blanching when I left the academy altogether. James deserves his own sentence, for many dinners and for not compelling me to read all of that Galperin book. Inger Brodey, and her daughters, Emma and Clara, were and remain far more wonderful than I can possibly conjure on the page. Claude Rawson, my undergraduate mentor, taught me to love *Persuasion*, and his counsel has remained indispensable in the years since.

I owe a great debt to John Knight and Emily Bell, my editors at Farrar, Straus and Giroux, and to Lisa Silverman, my copy editor. Mitzi Angel earned my undying gratitude and confusion when she first called to suggest a book, and my agent, Edward Orloff, deserves fresh roses for his work on my behalf.

Thanks, as well, to Evan Kindley, Audrey Bilger, and my other editors at the *Los Angeles Review of Books*; to Nick Jackson, Jennifer Sahn, Taylor Le, and Katie Kilkenny at *Pacific Standard* magazine; to Jane Yong Kim at the *Atlantic*; and to Sadie Stein at *The Paris Review*, where this book began. For their writerly criticism and friendly encouragement, I cannot here omit Anne Fadiman, Brian Reed, Dan Wilner, Michelle Legro, Sarah Boyd, Lindsay Starck, John Lingan, Lucia Graves, Angela Serratore, Anne Connell, Mike Riggs, Joe Fletcher, Jerrod Rosenbaum, and Jeff Winkler. Thanks also to Doug and Lani for helping watch the cat.

Thanks to Julia Matson for the tea and the laughs; to Prashansa Taneja for letting me give her dancing lessons; to Devoney Looser for being a star; to Syrie James and Diana Birchall for arranging the theatricals in Montréal; and to Adam, Ashley, Michele, and the rest of the summer-camp crew for their pioneering work in North Carolina. To Jade Papa, clothing historian and costume genius, I can only say: thanks for your patience.

As for my mother, there is little here to add. Each sentence is for her, and none would have been possible without her. Also, I'm glad she corrected me about the turkeys in *Emma*.